BUSINESS CON[T]
MANAGEMENT
In Practice

BCS, The Chartered Institute for IT

Our mission as BCS, The Chartered Institute for IT, is to enable the information society. We promote wider social and economic progress through the advancement of information technology science and practice. We bring together industry, academics, practitioners and government to share knowledge, promote new thinking, inform the design of new curricula, shape public policy and inform the public.

Our vision is to be a world-class organisation for IT. Our 70,000 strong membership includes practitioners, businesses, academics and students in the UK and internationally. We deliver a range of professional development tools for practitioners and employees. A leading IT qualification body, we offer a range of widely recognised qualifications.

Further Information

BCS, The Chartered Institute for IT
First Floor, Block D
North Star House, North Star Avenue
Swindon, SN2 1FA, United Kingdom
T +44 (0) 1793 417 424
F +44 (0) 1793 417 444
www.bcs.org/contactus

BUSINESS CONTINUITY MANAGEMENT
In Practice

Stuart Hotchkiss

Published by British Informatics Society Limited (BISL), a wholly owned subsidiary of BCS The Chartered Institute for IT First Floor, Block D, North Star House, North Star Avenue, Swindon, SN2 1FA, UK. www.bcs.org

ISBN 978-1-906124-72-4

British Cataloguing in Publication Data.
A CIP catalogue record for this book is available at the British Library.

Typeset by The Charlesworth Group.
Printed at CPI Antony Rowe, Chippenham, UK

CONTENTS

LIST OF FIGURES AND TABLES

ABOUT THE AUTHOR

Stuart Hotchkiss is a business consultant in Hewlett Packard Technology Services EMEA. He has over 30 years of experience in IT from many domains, of which the last 16 have been in security and business continuity. This book shares some of that experience. The opinions in it are his alone.

ABBREVIATIONS

AS	Australian Standards
ATM	Automated Teller Machine
BCM	Business Continuity Management
BCP	Business Continuity Planning
BIA	Business Impact Analysis
CIA	Confidentiality, Integrity and Availability (of data)
CPU	Central Processing Unit
DR	Disaster Recovery
HR	Human Resources
IEC	International Electrotechnical Commission
ISO	International Organization for Standardization
ITIL	Information Technology Infrastructure Library
ITSCM	IT Service Continuity Management
LAN	Local Area Network
LOB	Line of Business
MTO	Maximum Tolerable Outage
NZS	New Zealand Standard
P&L	Profit and Loss
RPO	Recovery Point Objective
RTC	Recovery Time Capability
RTO	Recovery Time Objective
SAN	Storage Area Network
SPOF	Single Point of Failure

GLOSSARY

Asset Physical items such as computer systems, vehicles and buildings. 'Resource' has a broader definition (see below).

Business Continuity Management (BCM) The process of developing and maintaining a complete business continuity plan which will ensure the continuity of a business when disruptions occur. BCM covers plan development based on the business impact analysis, the exercising of the plan and the regular updating of the plan to reflect new threats, risks and business circumstances.

Business Continuity Plan (BCP) The documented procedures defining what happens when risk scenarios materialise. The plan should cover all scenarios and procedures and act as guide when business disruption occurs. The business continuity plan is updated and maintained via the BCM process defined above.

Business Impact Analysis (BIA) This is the process of determining which areas of a business have potential losses requiring mitigation and what controls are needed. Controls can reduce or, occasionally, eliminate risk and loss. Controls cost money and, in a BIA, the objective is also to balance the cost of these with risk appetite. (Risk appetite is simply the tolerance for risk – some companies accept high risks, others don't.)

The output of a BIA should give sufficient information to company management to enable them to protect the critical resources needed to protect their revenues. The primary goal is to prioritise the revenue streams: this will automatically exclude some revenue streams and business processes from further analysis. (Here 'revenue' refers to real revenue or potential losses due to, for example, intangible factors like damaged reputations.)

Senior management must have information to decide:

- which business units, operations and processes are absolutely essential to the survival of the organisation;
- how quickly essential business units or processes have to be back in operation (i.e. at what point the impact is no longer tolerable);
- which recovery alternatives are the most plausible for meeting the recovery times;

- which resources are needed to resume operations at a survival level for the business;
- which elements must be implemented in advance in order to meet the recovery times;
- how much money to spend on risk mitigation.

Controls These are the countermeasures for vulnerabilities. There are four major types:

- deterrent controls to reduce the likelihood of a deliberate attack;
- preventative controls to protect against vulnerabilities and make an attack unsuccessful or reduce its impact;
- corrective controls to reduce the effect of an attack;
- detective controls to discover attacks and trigger preventative or corrective controls.

As an example of the above, a threat to a network can come from an external intrusion and render the assets (systems etc.) unusable. The vulnerability exists because of weaknesses in an operating system and the control is to introduce a firewall to filter traffic. Note that in this example the risk is not reduced to zero – it is mitigated by the control and reduced in impact only.

CPU Central processing unit – commonly known as a computer and synonymous with it.

Disaster Recovery (DR) In the context of this book this is a procedure for a scenario perceived to be a disaster. 'Disaster' is a subjective term. However DR is very often used within IT to mean the technical procedures and components in place to keep the IT function running when part of the IT infrastructure is out of commission. Commonly in IT it refers to moving processing from a main site to a secondary one for a limited time.

More broadly DR anticipates certain types of event which are dramatic in nature (such as fire in a building) and which require processing and personnel to move to alternate sites. For these latter two definitions there should still exist a procedure defining all the actions that need to take place. This is developed in advance of the disaster occurring.

Disruption The period during which some part of a business does not work as expected due to an event and the business stops. The duration of a disruption determines whether business continuity procedures need to be executed. If the disruption duration is shorter than the maximum tolerable outage (MTO) BCM procedures are not usually executed.

Event Something that happens – for example a fire in a building. It is of interest mainly due to its consequences (see 'Scenario').

Functional departments These are departments providing services to many others. IT is commonly a function as is Facilities. The issue here is that a weakness in a function affects many areas and improving functional performance and risk can be seen as a general improvement to the business ecosystem.

Governance The set of metrics including when they will be measured, who is responsible for each and which is used as a framework to apportion responsibility for BCM within an organisation. It ensures that every aspect of BCM has an 'owner' who can be held responsible and forms a communications framework making everyone in a business aware of BCM. As such it is a key component in making a BCM programme work.

Impact The loss when business cannot continue because of a disruption. Impact should always be expressed in monetary terms since it is used to determine whether it is worth investing in measures to avoid the disruption. The disruption can be avoided by having a procedure which either provides some alternative way of continuing in business or fixes the problem within an acceptable time. The impact does not always occur immediately after a disruption occurs and most businesses can survive for some time before losses start. This period is the MTO (see below) for the business and varies between companies and lines of business (LOBs).

Incident Management The process whereby incidents are reported and handled. Very often this is managed by some kind of service desk or call centre. Incident management is the focal point for all stakeholders and, in particular, served customers to report things not working as expected. As such, it will often be the means by which an event is discovered and should be tightly coordinated with escalation procedures and eventually, by management judgment, the implementation of a prewritten procedure for business continuity. Management judgment is essential when an incident escalates, since it may be that an exact procedure has not been documented and that some modifications should occur. It may even be that no BCM procedure exists, in which case management must gather together the subject area experts to solve the scenario and document what happens as a formal procedure to add to the library of BCM procedures. Failure to integrate incident management and business continuity management inevitably leads to longer recovery times or continuity plans which do not work in practice.

ITIL The Information Technology Infrastructure Library (ITIL) is a set of concepts and practices for Information Technology Services Management, Information Technology (IT) development and IT operations. ITIL gives detailed descriptions of a number of important IT practices and provides comprehensive checklists, tasks and procedures that any IT organisation can tailor to its needs.

IT Service Continuity Management (ITSCM) The processes by which plans are put in place and managed to ensure that IT services can recover and continue after an incident. ITSCM is part of ITIL but not a substitute for business continuity planning or management.

LAN Local area network or, in common usage, the network connecting all the printers, PCs and other IT equipment.

Line of business (LOB) This refers to a part of a business which generates revenue and has a management responsibility for it. The term is used generically. Some parts of a business may only generate cost and cross charge that cost to other parts. For example Internal Finance may charge its costs *pro rata* to business units based on revenue split. In this example Finance can be considered either a resource used by other areas (in which case it will feature in a resource mapping) or a unique area with its revenue being its internal cross charges. This depends entirely upon the company.

Mitigation The actions put in place to reduce the impact of a risk. In the context of this book 'mitigation' generally refers to a business continuity procedure which, when executed, will reduce business impact either by fixing a problem that occurs and allowing business to continue or providing an alternative way for it to continue. As an example if office space is not available due to a fire, either the fire can be put out and the office returned to use quickly or alternative office space can be used.

Maximum Tolerable Outage (MTO) How long things can fail to work before it becomes an issue. This is often subjective and a lot of stakeholders will say the maximum is minutes whereas a client might actually tolerate hours. The process of judging this is based upon experience.

Outage Synonymous with 'Disruption'.

Procedure A document defining the steps to be executed in chronological sequence when a given scenario occurs. There is one procedure for each scenario. A procedure defines what should happen in each step and who should execute it, together with an estimate of the time it should take. A procedure is used to test the reaction to a scenario and give an estimate of the recovery time capability when it occurs. A procedure should be sufficiently detailed to be executable by a person who is not an expert in the particular domain.

Recovery Time Objective (RTO) How quickly you would like to be able to get going again. Obviously this should be equal to or lower than the MTO. In general more emphasis should be placed on RTO (and the associated RTC, outlined below) than on RPO (see below). RTO is affected by people and processes, and requires careful planning and synchronisation, whereas RPO is largely affected by money. Customers are also affected more by RTO than anything else. RTO calculations are very often based on the recovery of IT and fail to look at the entire chain of events from a customer perspective. Commonly the IT part of a chain can recover in 15 minutes but the other parts (people and processes) take two hours.

Recovery Time Capability(RTC) How long it actually takes to get going again. Theoretically this should be less than or equal to the RTO but, in practice, it doesn't have to be, since good customer communications and planning of alternatives with the same or reduced service capability can often satisfy clients.

Recovery Point Objective (RPO) The loss of data or work when something stops working. An RPO of 30 minutes means that 30 minutes will be lost so, when work restarts, these 30 minutes of lost work or data need to be handled in some way. An RPO is never zero in practice except for some very specialised and expensive methods of data handling. Given that all companies use double entry accounting systems, arguably an RPO of zero is never a requirement.

Risks These are things that go wrong, together with their impact. Usually they are described without reference to the impact, since it is assumed there is such an impact. For example 'Building access denied due to smoke damage'. For each risk like this there should be a scenario and procedure. A risk materialises when the threat occurs. A threat occurs with a frequency such as a number of times per year and this gives the probability of the threat occurring. The risk is the multiple of the impact and the probability: a high impact threat with a very low probability probably carries the same risk level as a low impact risk with a medium probability.

Risk assessment Where threats are seen as serious enough to warrant further investigation, this process looks at the probability of their occurrence to come up with a risk.

Resources Things a business or line of business needs to function, such as:

- applications used by business;
- people;
- real estate;
- support functions like HR and Finance;
- IT infrastructure;
- business partners or suppliers.

Storage Area Network (SAN) A way of having lots of storage distributed around a network so that systems neither know nor care where it is. If it doesn't work or breaks in some way then the result is that lots of other things can't work properly, such as all the computers on the network and all the applications people use.

Scenario A description of an event and its consequences which a stakeholder can use to help him or her plan accordingly. For the event 'Fire in a building' a typical scenario would be 'Office space unavailable due to a fire in the building'.

A stakeholder can start to develop a plan of action when a scenario occurs and this will be documented as a procedure. In this example we expect a stakeholder to plan what he would do if his office space were unavailable. We would not expect him to deal with the event and write a procedure to put out the fire.

All scenarios should focus on a description that defines the consequences of an event rather than the event itself. In this example many events could lead to office space being unavailable.

Stakeholders Anybody involved in or affected by business continuity planning development. The BCM project manager and his team, those management representatives who are interviewed in the BIA, the functional department managers and their staff are the main stakeholders in most cases.

Threats These are things that can go wrong or 'attack' the organisation. Examples might include fire or fraud. Threats are ever-present. They can apply to people, processes, physical assets, buildings and components etc. If unmitigated a threat can cause business disruption.

Threat analysis Looking at the threats to a business and determining which are realistic and should be looked at in more detail. As an example a plague of locusts is a threat to any business anywhere but would not be retained as a realistic threat in Siberia in the winter. Sometimes this process is called 'risk analysis'. However it is confusing and inconsistent and does not align with the way ordinary people think.

Vulnerabilities These make an organisation more susceptible to a threat or make an attack more likely to have a harmful impact. For example fire vulnerability would be the presence of inflammable materials such as paper.

PREFACE

I wrote this book as a result of running projects for customers and seeing the huge difference between what is required and what is preached. Initially I thought it was me who didn't understand the subject but, when I noticed how many businesses have no plans of any sort and how many of the remainder have none of any merit, I started to think that perhaps there was either a disinterest in the subject or it was being made so complex that the methods used could never lead to a workable plan in a reasonable time.

I decided to document the core actions that need to be taken using common sense – not just my own but that gathered from customers trying to come up with plans that can be tested and work.

Immediately some issues became obvious:

- Stakeholder support at every level is more important than management support. Having management support is a requirement, otherwise there will be no money, but no company works by dictatorship. Getting things done in practice is easier once stakeholders are sold on the idea than when they are forced to do something because management says so.

- Using the traditional shock tactics to scare people into having plans doesn't work. There is no point in saying the losses will be huge if something happens because the numbers are simply beyond understanding. Business continuity is more easily understandable if it is sold simply as a means of being efficient in the face of a failure and not having to waste time, effort and money on what could have been planned in advance.

- Trying to have a plan for every event is not needed because some events can be absorbed and the risk taken. Every event should be considered and the decision to reject some and retain others should be conscious and documented.

- Having a plan for disasters but not for anything else. A disaster is usually seen to be something of high impact but very low probability or an IT issue. Neither of these is correct, and certainly not when there are no plans in place for certainties such as staff absence or equipment failure.

- Confusing threats with risks – there is a difference and risks can only be gauged when the chances of them happening (their probability) are known. There is no objective mathematical data of any use for risks, frankly, so it becomes a question of judgment. This is not something to be ashamed of – indeed it is a management requirement.

- Using tools which automate parts of the management cycle often causes more harm than good and the tool takes over to the point that running the tool is considered to be continuity planning. It isn't. Keep it simple.

- Following one of the dozens of standards doesn't help – it is fairly obvious what has to be done and a standard is not needed to tell you this. What is needed are practical steps to achieve the objective and the objective is not conformance to a standard but having a plan that people can execute and support when things go wrong – hence this book.

PREAMBLE

In theory, there is no difference between theory and practice but, in practice, there is...
Yogi Berra (Lawrence Peter 'Yogi' Berra (born 12 May 1925) is a former American Major League Baseball player and manager)

Everyone believes in the need for continuity in business. However the vast majority of businesses are unprepared for breakdowns, and those that are prepared have plans which are usually out of date. Businesses are prepared in the sense that they would do something differently from normal, but the essence of good continuity is that everything is planned in advance down to the smallest detail so that there is no need to think when something goes wrong.

There are multiple reasons for this lack of detailed planning but the key ones seem to be over-analysis of the business and a focus on IT only. IT is clearly the basis of every business, so it needs to be a core part of the equation. However IT has created an illusion that availability will solve everything, even though this is demonstrably not true. The issue of availability as a measure and an illusion is discussed in more detail later in the document.

The key to BCM is simplicity combined with planning for keeping the key parts (not all parts) of the business running at service levels that customers accept. This service level can be much lower than customers contracted for if the right measures are taken in terms of communications. BCM should aim at doing as much pre-planning as possible for probable events and plan for alternative ways to continue in business rather than adopting a simple break/fix attitude. There is almost always an alternative. For example if the invoicing application breaks down, it could be done by hand in some cases.

Over-analysis of impact and risks leads to paralysis and project plans lasting years – by which time the original project sponsors have changed and support may have been lost. Multiple milestones and short-term deliverables are the keys to keeping attention and being seen to be of value to the organisation.

Financing BCM is always an issue and the traditional approach is to use big numbers of potential losses to justify doing something. This should be avoided since it is simply not credible. BCM wins when it is easy and improves overall business efficiency in a reasonable timeframe.

Standards cause as much damage as good. They are reasonable checklists but none say how to do concrete things in a reasonable level of detail. What you will not find in this book is a treatise on how to implement any standard or framework.

This book takes a practical approach to the core issues and shows how to resolve them simply – if it isn't simple, it won't work. It is a recipe book based on experience and live projects which should satisfy all stakeholders and shows that practice is quite simple in comparison with theory. It is designed to provide all of the essential elements needed for any business, regardless of size, to implement a business continuity capability. It will provide all of the steps with enough detail to be able to tailor and implement the step for a business. It is designed to be simple but to cover everything. Everything in the book is based on real-life projects and works in practice.

What you will not find in this book is an overview of the types of technologies which can be used in the development of the IT side of a continuity capability. The technologies are well-known and their limitations and advantages are clear. Choosing the technology is usually constrained by costs, with the drive being for the cheapest. The key factor, of course, is to execute a proper Business Impact Analysis to agree the budget that can be justified – once this is clear the technology choice is clear. Most often this is not done and there is no real agreement, and the technology discussion is made complex as a result. Rather than review technologies which are well documented elsewhere, the focus here is on the process of developing the continuity capability.

INTRODUCTION AND PURPOSE

WHY HAVE BUSINESS CONTINUITY?

At first this may seem to be an idiotic question. No company can afford to stop being in business so something should be done to ensure this doesn't happen. The question becomes: 'What should be done and how do you pay for it?'

There are some events that every business will try to avoid or plan for. Typically continuity plans for these events are paid for by an expression of the risk of monetary loss and then an expression of a reasonable amount to mitigate this loss. If there is a high probability of an event happening every year and the cost of the event is 1 million pounds, then a budget of 50,000 pounds to mitigate or, better, avoid this sounds reasonable. This is risk mitigation, which is usually the prime driver for having a continuity plan.

However another way to look at this question is to look at business efficiency. No matter what is done, there are always events which will cause business outage and they cannot be avoided completely. It makes more sense to plan for these certainties so that they are handled as efficiently as possible. Pre-planning is the essence of continuity and a pre-planned procedure defining what is to be done when something happens can be executed more quickly than the normal confusion which arises when no planning is done.

Business continuity needs to be viewed from these two angles to be effective.

WHAT EXACTLY IS A 'CONTINUITY PLAN'?

A continuity plan is just a collection of things you do when something goes wrong. For each potential risk there should be a procedure (or plan) to be executed to get you out of the mess. Note that the measure is impact, not the loss of the asset. For example a small disc crash on a computer which costs nothing to repair can cause immeasurable impact and damage if the data it holds is important and there is no mitigation for its loss (mitigation could be some form of backup, for example).

Small impact events can also cause damage in terms of time to repair. A small part failing when there are no spares in stock can cause a fairly limited impact on business but can cost a lot of money to repair because of a lack of planning. This means that you need to consider the impact and the damage as well as the recovery cost to come to a reasonable idea of the cost of not having a continuity plan.

A business continuity plan is simply a document which breaks down (or should) into all the little sub-plans (or procedures) to execute when things go wrong. Often reference is made to 'continuity plans' (plural) – in this book they are called procedures and the collection of procedures plus supporting data is the business continuity plan.

A continuity plan can be a specific plan for the failure of either an individual part of a business (such as a product line or service) or a physical area (site) where the impact affects many lines of business.

The site failure is the most common view of what a business continuity plan should be but this is erroneous because it leads to the idea that continuity is only about site failure and moving to alternative sites or using alternative sites. Site failure represents a tiny proportion of the outages which cause business impact.

BUSINESS CONTINUITY – PLANNING OR MANAGEMENT?

What is the difference? These terms are often used interchangeably, which adds to the confusion. Worse, many businesses (the majority) have plans but no management, so their plans are out of date.

As previously stated a business continuity plan is a collection of the documented procedures that should be followed when things go wrong. There will be a procedure for every risk retained by the business and no procedures for those not retained. The procedures should work in most cases as long as the risk materialises in the exact form expected – this may not happen, of course. A risk could be expected to materialise in a form such as '50% of staff are absent' – if it turns out that 80% are absent then some plans might need to be adapted. It could also be that a new risk occurs which was unforeseen and for which there is no plan (no procedure). In this case one has to be improvised, or a similar one used with some modifications. It is most important that, when this happens, the new risk and new procedure are formalised and included in the plans for the future. This leads to the need for business continuity management.

Business continuity management is the lifecycle of:

- looking at business impact on a regular basis;
- reviewing risks on a regular basis;
- updating or designing procedures in the light of new risk, changed risks or changes to the resources needed for a procedure;
- communicating with staff and training all staff regularly;
- testing plans regularly;
- auditing regularly.

Miss any of these steps (all explained in detail later) and you have a plan but no management, which means that the plan will eventually fail. Plan failure means not passing audit, disappointing customers and taking longer than needed to resolve outage problems. Taking longer might mean either resolving a problem in 30 minutes instead of 10 or a very long outage. As a simple example imagine that, because of a lack of planning, no vendors were obliged to have continuous support plans and you have a problem obtaining support where you have priority over others – the consequences could be dire.

WHY DOES CONTINUITY MANAGEMENT FAIL?

The failure of a continuity plan has many effects but the major one is taking longer than needed to get back to business after an outage. The time taken is one issue but the cost can be exorbitant in some cases.

As an example, if a continuity plan requires the movement of work from one location to another it should also document how to move it back and re-establish the original state. It is all too easy to have a lower priority for this part of the plan because the real problem is getting going again.

The failure of an individual plan is something that can be corrected relatively easily – by following this book for example – but the failure of the continuity management capability is more complex. The principal reasons for failure are these:

- Not executing an impact analysis. The results are that the right budget is not allocated, the focus is on part of the business or some of the resources (IT being the most flagrant example) and management and stakeholders don't understand or agree with what is being done.

- Not understanding the time commitment. The initial development of a continuity management capability will take a lot of time (at least a year) but there is then an ongoing commitment to keep the plan up-to-date and test it. These timescales give plenty of opportunity for the focus to be lost and for the stakeholders to forget.

- Not understanding the advantages. A continuity capability has advantages to a business in terms of efficiency and market competitiveness and advantages to customers of the business. If neither of these is fully understood and communicated, the continuity capability will often be seen only as a cost for events which are unlikely, or whose consequences have been overdramatised.

A REAL-LIFE CONTINUITY PLAN

Let's take a simple situation which needs to have a plan. In practice this is probably never done but, after reading this, you might change your mind.

Here is the situation. You have a house and live in it with your wife and two children. The children are old enough to be left at home alone for a while but are not young adults or adolescents so they may not show the kind of initiative you would expect at that age. In other words things need to be spelled out.

3

You go out for the afternoon and are located two hours away – too far away to return to fix a problem immediately. The problem is that there is a water leak and it affects your prize tropical fish so it needs to be stopped as well as fixed. The kids call you (at least they have your contact details...) and tell you. Your reaction is to tell them to shut off the water supply and call the plumber.

Their first reaction is, 'Where is the supply shut off valve?' Answer: 'In the cellar.' My cellar has six rooms, so which one is it in and where is it exactly? They find it and then ask how to switch it off – do you turn it to the right or the left and, if so, how far? (Incidentally turning a tap to the right or the left is self-evident to some people and a complete mystery to others.) They succeed in turning off the water supply and now must rescue the tropical fish, which need a continuous supply of fresh water and can survive for one hour maximum without it, so you can't race home in time.

Two things need to be done now. They need to get a plumber and they may also need to put some other contingency plan in place for the fish. You tell them to call the plumber. They want to know who the plumber is and how to contact him, of course. After they look up his number they call and he is out, so there is no reply and therefore the plumbing company cannot recommend who else could do the job. Who do the kids contact now?

I think you probably get the picture already and realise that what you really need is a plan like this:

Table I.1 Event: Water leak

Steps	Methods	Comments
Switch off the water supply to the house	The tap is in the cellar next to the hot water boiler, is coloured green and has a meter on it. It is the only one	Turn it to the right until it won't go any further. Flush a toilet and make sure it doesn't fill to check if the water is switched off. If not, keep turning to the right
Call the plumber	Mr Jones from Plumbalot: 034 997 2167	Tell him it is urgent because of the fish and I will pay the premium. If he is not there call another service (next)
Call the emergency plumbing service	034 274 3344	Tell them it is urgent and you need it done in an hour
Prepare to move the fish	Get buckets from the garage (on the shelf)	Just get ready. If the plumber comes within an hour, do nothing. If not, call me and then put the fish in the buckets etc.

The last step is fantasy, of course, but you get the idea. In this simple script the kids don't need to think about anything, they just follow the instructions. The phone numbers are already known and everything is clear. Business continuity planning for business events is no different.

OUTAGES IN PRACTICE

Things go wrong and there are a limited number of things that can be done to stop this, so the thing to do is to deal with this by planning in advance. For example you cannot legislate against staff sometimes being late – they will be late due to circumstances beyond their control. You cannot avoid things breaking down or illness or fires or suppliers having similar problems.

The graphic below is a common one from the IT world. It shows the sources of outages or breakdowns in a typical business. A continuity capability must address all of the sources of outage, otherwise a plan won't work. It is very common to address site disasters but not to address other sources of certain failure, such as application failure or staff illness

As an example, it is surprising how much money is spent avoiding the possibility of fire (which is not certain) but how little is spent avoiding or planning for certain failure. Examples of certain failure are many. Transport will be late. Operating systems and applications will fail. People will not do as they are told. Instructions will always have some ambiguity. The list is endless but little is done to plan for workarounds in advance of them happening. Business continuity is assured by planning alternative methods of working, as well as by trying to avoid risks entirely or just fixing problems when they occur.

Figure I.1 Causes of outages

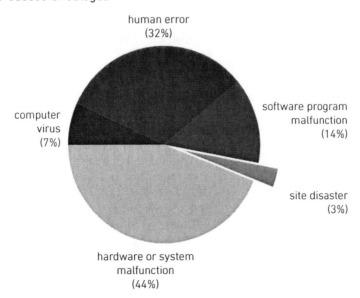

Business continuity planning is about planning in advance for failure. It is also ensuring that the service levels (in the broadest sense) are maintained to keep customers satisfied. This does not mean that the service level remains the same – the level of service a customer will be happy with is directly related to how the service level is perceived. A customer who is kept informed about problems in a very direct way will remain a customer in the long term even if the actual service is very bad; a customer who has been ignored will leave even when the service level is only slightly lower than expected.

A great deal of business continuity is about communication. We really need to start from the point that problems are going to happen and plan how to deal with them. Fixing a problem is not the whole solution. In this context, 'fixing' means getting back to the state before the problem occurred. Problem 'fixing' is one part of business continuity planning – the key point is to plan alternative ways of doing things too. As a very simple example, if the invoicing function in a company breaks down there are a number of ways of continuing to invoice: doing it by hand, repairing the broken system or sending the invoice data to a service bureau. Each has a cost. Each has advantages and disadvantages but each ought to be considered.

The overall philosophy here is that the essence of continuity planning is planning in detail for certain failure and driving this via the people who operate the business by asking them to design everyday scenarios for each risk identified. These scenarios can be tested and updated as risks evolve and will generally improve the efficiency of a business by reducing any time and effort wasted on panic or confusion when outages occur. Given that the overwhelming majority of outages are small, we could expect that this type of planning would already be in place, but experience shows this not to be true.

THE BCM LIFECYCLE

Business continuity starts with an expression of the strategic intent of a company to include continuity in its regulatory capabilities or as some kind of competitive differentiator. A BCM policy document is then drawn up as part of the implementation mechanism. Once these two basic documents are produced, approved and communicated, the lifecycle of management can start.

The following steps are the basic requirements of a business continuity capability. Note that the cycle does not end and represents a high-level view of the major steps needed to develop a practical capability in business continuity.

Figure I.2 Lifecycle of business continuity capability

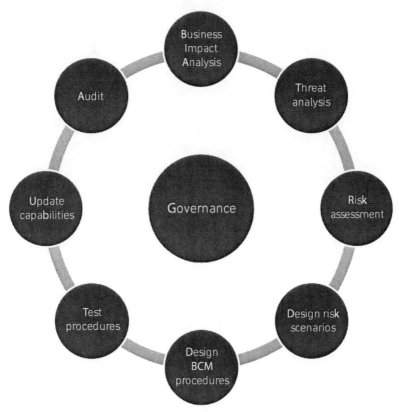

Business Impact Analysis: Analyses the business and determines which parts have a sufficiently high impact that there is a need to mitigate the risks with continuity capabilities, amongst others.

Threat analysis: This is done by two groups: the line of business leaders will give their views of threats during the BIA interviews and then the underlying functions upon which they depend will give their views. These two views are consolidated to give a general picture of the threats and the current countermeasures. Only the unmitigated threats should go through for risk assessment and scenario development.

Risk assessment: Once the threats are identified there is a need for a further analysis of the risks they represent. This step involves looking at the probability of each risk together with its impact.

Design risk scenarios: Management proposes scenarios which are reflections of the potential risks determined by the BIA. Scenarios are simple expressions of a failure such as, 'Access to a building denied for six hours'.

Design BCM procedures: This involves documenting testable procedures to execute when the risk scenarios occur. A procedure is a set of steps to execute in sequence to achieve continuity – whether this is an alternative way of working or a means of bringing back the pre-outage situation.

Test procedures: Tests the procedures and determines if they work, and how long they will take to execute when one of the risk scenarios occurs.

Update capabilities: As a result of testing, the actual capabilities may be better or worse than expected and these results should be judged and used in whichever expression of contract is used (such as a product capability or a service level agreement).

Audit: Typically capabilities will be audited on a regular basis, leading to both corrective action and a new Business Impact Analysis.

The central module of this lifecycle represents the concept of governance of the continuity capability. It is something which is done at every stage of the lifecycle and which affects many people during the lifecycle continuously. Good governance frameworks will ensure that everybody has some kind of metric to achieve in support of business continuity.

All of the above concepts are developed in more detail later in this document. However **the key to success is defining what steps should be taken when risk scenarios occur and making sure that the scenarios are related to risks perceived and developed by the people running the business on a daily basis**. This method will provide scenarios which are understood, which have probably happened (or easily could), and the procedures for which can be tested.

As a simple example of the process:

Table I.2 Assessing a risk scenario

Impact analysis	If we lose production line suppliers the impact is £500,000 per month
Threat analysis	Threats are weather, strikes, suppliers' lack of plans, loss of personnel
Risk assessment	Acceptable provisions are in place against all threats, with the exceptions of suppliers' lack of plans and personnel loss. These two factors have high impact and high probability
Example risk scenario 1	Supplier A is on strike for one week
Example risk scenario 2	Supplier B delivers one hour late due to snow

For each scenario, design a set of steps to handle the scenario. For example, in the case of scenario 1, look at alternative suppliers with which we made arrangements in advance, and for which there is an increased cost for short delivery with little notice. The steps would simply involve contacting the alternative supplier, sending order details, arranging shipments, organising stocking in case it is different etc. These steps would be set up in advance. The supplier would know in advance that it is an alternative supplier and a contract would be set up with terms and conditions and delivery plans etc. Simple planning.

Try to negotiate a clause in the original supplier's contract to reduce our financial impact as a general mitigation of impact. For scenario 2 propose keeping extra stock to cover such a delay, or simply have a plan to communicate with clients. Remember that continuity plans do not necessarily mean no impact and conditions identical to those prior to an event.

1 GENERAL ISSUES IN CONTINUITY MANAGEMENT

There are many preconceived ideas in the world of continuity planning which will be addressed here.

SOME TERMINOLOGY

Unfortunately there are some specific terms used in this domain which tend to have rather esoteric meanings and which can complicate discussions. The fundamental question that is usually asked is, 'How long will it take to get going again?' If this time is such that a client won't notice then this is good; if it takes longer and the client does notice then maybe something should be done to reduce the time it takes. In this area there is always a balance between capability and objective. The common terms used are these:

MTO – maximum tolerable outage: How long things can be broken before it becomes an issue. This is often subjective and a lot of stakeholders will say the maximum is minutes whereas a client might actually tolerate hours. The process of judging this is based upon experience.

RTO – recovery time objective: How long you would like to take to get going again. Obviously this should be equal to or less than the MTO. In general more emphasis should be placed on RTO (and the associated RTC below) than on RPO (see below). RTO is affected by people and processes and requires careful planning and synchronisation, whereas RPO is largely affected by money. Customers are also more affected by RTO than anything else. RTO calculations are very often based on the recovery of IT and fail to look at the entire chain of events from a customer perspective. It is common to hear that the IT part of a chain can recover in 15 minutes but the other parts (people and processes) take two hours.

RTC – recovery time capability: How long it actually takes to get going again. Theoretically this should be less than or equal to the RTO but, in practice, it doesn't have to be, since good customer communications and planning of alternatives with the same or reduced service capability can often satisfy clients.

RPO – recovery point objective: When something stops working, data or work is lost. An RPO of 30 minutes means that 30 minutes will be lost so, when work restarts, these 30 minutes of lost work or data need to be handled in some way. An RPO is never zero in practice except for some very specialised and expensive methods of data handling. Given that all companies use double entry accounting systems, arguably an RPO of zero is never a requirement.

Threats: These are things that can go wrong or 'attack' the organisation. Examples might include fire or fraud. Threats are ever-present for every organisation. Threats can apply to people, processes, physical assets, buildings and components etc. A threat, if unmitigated, can cause business disruption – threats that do not cause disruption directly or indirectly do not need to be considered here.

Risks: These are things that go wrong, together with their impact. Usually they are described without reference to the impact, since it is assumed there is such an impact. For example, 'Building access denied due to smoke damage'. For each risk like this there should be a scenario and procedure to execute.

Resources: Things a business or line of business needs to function, such as, but not limited to:

- applications used by business;
- people;
- real estate;
- support functions like HR and Finance;
- IT infrastructure;
- business partners or suppliers.

Vulnerabilities: These make an organisation more prone to attack by a threat or make an attack more likely to have some success or impact. For example fire vulnerability would be the presence of inflammable materials (such as paper).

Controls: These are the countermeasures for vulnerabilities. There are four major types that should be present:

- deterrent controls to reduce the likelihood of a deliberate attack;
- preventative controls to protect vulnerabilities and make an attack unsuccessful or reduce its impact;
- corrective controls to reduce the effect of an attack;
- detective controls to discover attacks and trigger preventative or corrective controls.

As an example of the above, a **threat** to a network can come from an external intrusion and render the **assets** (systems etc.) unusable. The **vulnerability** exists because of weaknesses in an operating system and the **control** is to introduce a firewall to filter traffic. Note that in this example the risk is not reduced to zero – it is **mitigated** by the **control** and reduced in impact only.

Business Impact Analysis (BIA): This is the process of determining which areas of a business have potential losses requiring mitigation and what controls are needed. Controls can reduce or, occasionally, eliminate risk and loss. Controls cost money and, in a BIA, the objective is also to balance the cost of controls with risk appetite. (Risk appetite is simply the tolerance for risk – some companies accept high risks, others don't.)

The output of a BIA should give sufficient information to company management to enable them to take actions to protect the critical resources needed to protect their revenues and reduce the risk to revenue. The primary goal is to prioritise the revenue streams – this will automatically exclude some revenue streams and business processes from further analysis. (Here 'revenue' refers to real revenue or potential losses due to, for example, intangible factors like damaged reputations.)

Senior management must have information to decide:

- which business units, operations and processes are absolutely essential to the survival of the organisation;
- how quickly essential business units or processes have to be back in operation (i.e. at what point the impact is no longer tolerable);
- which recovery alternatives are the most plausible for meeting the recovery times;
- which resources are needed to resume operations at a survival level for the essential parts of the business;
- which elements must be pre-positioned in order to meet the recovery times;
- how much money to spend on risk mitigation.

Line of business: This refers to a part of a business which generates revenue and which has a manager responsible for that revenue. It is used generically. Some parts of a business may only generate cost and cross charge that cost to other parts of the business. For example Internal Finance may charge its costs *pro rata* to business units based on revenue split. In this example Finance can be considered to be either a resource used by other areas (so it will feature in a resource mapping) or a unique area with its revenue being its internal cross charges. This depends entirely upon the company organisation.

Functional departments: These are departments which provide services to many others. IT is commonly a function, as is Facilities. The issue here is that a weakness in a function affects many areas and improving functional performance and risk can be seen as a general improvement to the business ecosystem.

Stakeholders: Anybody involved in business continuity planning development. So the project manager and his team, those management representatives who are interviewed in the BIA, the functional department managers and their staff are the main stakeholders in most cases.

STANDARDS

There are many standards and guidelines which cover the topic of business continuity, but only two will be mentioned here since they are the most common and encompass the others. The major issue is that they tell you what to do but not how to do it. In a lot of cases it is quite possible to comply with some standard but have no objective capability when it comes to business resistance to failure. Unfortunately this is increasingly common.

BS25999

The main player is BS25999. This has not yet been approved as a standard by ISO, although it does cover just about everything that other 'standards' cover. The general objective of a standard should be that if you conform to it then (i) your business is comparable with others which conform and (ii) conformance brings automatic alignment between need and ability. Neither of these is true with BS25999. As a result it is a reasonably useful checklist to make sure nothing is missed out, but you can get this from this book instead and it will be easier to understand and implement.

The BS25999 site (www.bs25999.com) states:

> *BS25999 is a standard that establishes the process, principles and terminology of business continuity management. The standard deals with broad goals and is therefore non prescriptive so as to make it applicable to small and large business and local or global organizations.*

Part 1 is a code of practice and Part 2 is the specification.

Whenever you see the words 'code of practice', 'guidelines' or 'recommendation' this indicates an opinion, rather than anything that can be followed towards an end objective. BS25999 is deliberately generic to make it applicable to any customer or business. Therein lies the problem.

ITSCM – IT Service Continuity Management

This is not a standard as such but a major section of ITIL which covers the continuity of IT services. In most cases this happens to be the pivot on which business runs, so it has a high relevance. As such it is of limited use for business continuity, since it only covers IT and assumes that the IT is organised around a 'services' philosophy, which may not always be the case.

Wikipedia gives the following description (as of 7 September 2010):

> *IT Service Continuity management covers the processes by which plans are put in place and managed to ensure that IT Services can recover and continue even after a serious incident occurs. It is not just about reactive measures, but also about proactive measures – reducing the risk of a disaster in the first instance.*
>
> *Continuity management is regarded by the application owners as the recovery of the IT infrastructure used to deliver IT Services, but as of 2009 many businesses practice the much further-reaching process of Business Continuity Planning (BCP), to ensure that the whole end-to-end business process can continue should a serious incident occur (at primary support level).*
>
> *Continuity management involves the following basic steps:*
>
> - *prioritising the activities to be recovered by conducting a Business Impact Analysis (BIA);*
> - *performing a Risk Assessment (aka risk analysis) for each of the IT Services to identify the assets, threats, vulnerabilities and countermeasures for each service;*
> - *evaluating the options for recovery;*
> - *producing the Contingency Plan;*
> - *testing, reviewing, and revising the plan on a regular basis.*

Continuity management involves the following basic steps:

- prioritising the business areas to be recovered by conducting a Business Impact Analysis (BIA);
- performing a risk assessment (a.k.a. risk analysis) for each of the IT services to identify the assets, threats, vulnerabilities and countermeasures for each service;
- evaluating the options for recovery;
- producing the contingency plan;
- testing, reviewing, and revising the plan on a regular basis.

So on the face of it this does everything…. What does it not do then?

The focus is on IT, which is not sufficient. Most IT infrastructures are pretty resilient anyway and most datacentres these days are built to decent standards. IT is only part of the problem. By focusing on IT the support of business is lost – only the technological dimensions of problems, and their resolution by technologists, are addressed.

Why the focus on serious incidents and disasters? The costs of small outages far outweigh those associated with 'disasters'. In addition customers are tolerant in the event of a disaster and usually don't even expect a decent level of service. However they are far less tolerant of simple inefficiency where there is no obvious reason things don't work. As a classic example, if a procedure is written to recover something and one of the phone numbers is wrong and it takes 10 minutes to get the right one, this is the downtime of a Class 4 datacentre for an **entire year**! Think about it.... What if this is all that is needed and not the entire ITIL framework? The vast majority of businesses do not use and have no need for ITIL.

ITSCM clearly defines the need, for example, to do a Business Impact Analysis but, in common with other frameworks, it doesn't tell you how to do it. In practice this is left to the imagination of the practitioner or, worse, a tool of some description, which then takes on a life of its own. If you want a continuity capability, don't rely solely on ITSCM or ITIL.

REGULATORY ISSUES

There are regulations in every industry which cover the need to have a business continuity capability. This stems from the basic concept of the due diligence which a company director (i.e. any functional manager) has as a responsibility to shareholders. This can be expressed as the requirement that the director looks after the assets of the company to maximise the shareholders' profits and, as such, would be negligent if the company went out of business due to some failure.

Within some industries this is more prescriptive and regulators and auditors will look for evidence of planning, but that is all they will look for. They will not look for compliance to any standard (except that the compliance can be seen as evidence) and they will not look for evidence of the risk level. This means that a company can clearly state that it has no plan in one or all areas because it has decided, and the shareholders have agreed, to take the risk. Regulators and auditors may have an opinion on the degree of risk taken, but there is no legislation against risk-taking.

This is not black and white. Listing the regulatory requirements here will not particularly help with making a plan work or implementing it, or in ensuring continuity. However regulatory requirements will have significant input in the design of a business continuity capability.

AVAILABILITY, UPTIME AND RELIABLE COMPONENTS

These remain a big focus in most organisations. At all levels management truly believe that availability is directly related to continuity and that, if availability is kept high via technology solutions, the problems of continuity are solved. The situation is exacerbated by measuring availability and uptime, and relating all metrics and service level agreements to these numbers. Indeed many frameworks cite this measure even in continuity planning.

This idea is patently false, which can be illustrated by a simple example. Modern planes are built with high quality, certified and tested components. They are rigorously tested and their availability (excluding scheduled maintenance) is near to 100% and probably higher than that achievable with computer systems. So why are planes sometimes late and why do they crash? If availability were the measure then this should not happen.

These events occur because the plane is one component in the chain of service to the final customer. Pilot error, air traffic control and variations in the weather are external factors which can cause a breakdown in customer service. The situation is exactly the same in any modern business. IT and the availability of any single component in the chain are not sufficient. Even if IT and other parts of the chain are all 100% available, this is no guarantee that unforeseen events will not destroy it.

Availability of components is important as a risk reduction measure. However it neither is nor should be the basis for any kind of service level agreement with customers. Extending the example shows the reason – if a customer turns up at check-in and his plane is late, saying that the plane has high availability will not satisfy him. However saying that the plane is going to be late but giving an alternative will provide some satisfaction.

To follow this example the availability syndrome leads to another issue. This is that the usual conclusion is to try to repair something which is broken (to shorten the downtime) rather than to provide an alternative. A plane which is late is usually **not** repaired – instead an alternative is provided, in the form of another type of transport, another plane or the provision of hotels (if the delay is long). These are all alternative methods of providing some customer service since it is neither realistic nor necessary to have a back-up plane on standby for every one in service.

This thinking should guide continuity plans in all business. Customer service (= revenue) should be the driver.

THE DOWNTIME MYTH

The cost of downtime is commonly bandied around in business continuity. It actually has little direct relevance even when it is measured correctly.

We find two broad ways of assessing the cost of downtime. One bases the calculation upon IT costs and looks at the costs of personnel, machines and so on. The other takes a broader view and tries to calculate the costs when business can't be done and then combines direct costs with revenue loss figures. The end result of either method adds little or no value to the discussion of business continuity.

This can be illustrated by analogy. If we had a factory making steel and it was 'down' for 30 minutes, restarting it would be relatively cheap. If it was down for three hours things would be different – molten steel cannot be kept for that length of time and suppliers would have to stop deliveries of new materials for example. All of these things would mean that to restart would not just be a simple process, but would require a degree of planning and rework. The cost of restarting increases over time.

In an IT 'factory' it is slightly different. If all of IT is concentrated in a datacentre, the datacentre can be switched on and off quite easily and the cost of restarting does not increase a great deal over time. Restarting means switching machines back on and recovering data and possibly some staff costs, but not much else.

In either of these cases, though, we can come up with a formula that says, 'The cost of downtime per hour (i.e. the cost of restarting) is X for the first two hours then Y after that,' for example. What does this tell us? Nothing – it is not relevant to business continuity.

If the cost of downtime is X per hour and we are down for two hours, does this cost 2X? Yes, but if the business has determined that it can tolerate being down for two hours then this cost is not a relevant measure.

APPLICATION AND ASSET MANAGEMENT

Here are two approaches which are rife with danger. Neither is of much practical use in the development of a business continuity plan.

In an asset-based approach, a risk analysis and assessment is done on an asset basis and mitigations are applied to those assets at the most risk. The assets are usually tangible (like plant). The theory is that if all the risks to all the assets are mitigated then the business faces no risk and continuity is assured. The problem arises when the assets considered don't cover all of the actual assets in a line of business and the chain of events (people and processes) connecting assets is not considered or mitigated. The majority of business outages do not arise because of a failure of assets but come from failures of people and processes.

In an application approach the idea is that, since businesses rely 100% on IT applications, if all these applications are reliable, the business is reliable and continuity is assured. The problems here include those of the asset approach, with the additional consideration of application interdependency. If application A requires application B then B failing will cause A to fail. The results can be very complex and provide more data than can be used to make a decision. If chains of applications were separated in such a way that they could be run on separated IT functions the situation would improve, but this is almost never the case so the underlying common denominator approach should be used and IT treated as a functional department.

Another thing to remember in the application approach is that applications are bound to fail, as are the systems upon which they run (including the operating system). Since failure is guaranteed, continuity must consider these scenarios and in particular the approach whereby what the application provided is done by alternative means.

IT WON'T HAPPEN TO US

Yes, it will. The classic excuse is, 'It happened last year so it won't happen again'. If this were true then you could buy your car, wreck it and then drive uninsured for the next twenty years certain that you would not have another accident because you have already had your share. You would not believe how many people think like this but try to explain that to your insurance company!

Another excuse: 'If it does happen then we have massive costs, so the money spent on any form of mitigation is a waste of money anyway. Why not just wait for it to happen and then only pay that?'

On the face of it this could almost be true. If a certain event happens regularly and you can't avoid it then it would be true, but events don't happen regularly and you can avoid them by planning. Why insure your car if an accident could mean you would lose the entire value of the car? The reasons are obvious – the car will not be entirely lost (the insurance will always pay some money back to you) and there are events which will cause losses which far exceed the value of the car (like hitting a more expensive car and it being your fault). This is the case in business too.

It is true that some companies insure themselves and their employees against, for example, accidents in hire cars. This is reasonable after an impact analysis has been done but as a general rule it is not.

Another excuse is the view that people work differently in a disaster so there is no need to plan procedures because they won't be followed anyway. This is the 'blitz' mentality. Can a business really be efficient if the actions to take during an outage are governed by no-one and unplanned? It is true that a lot of rules can and should be broken when outages occur but some modicum of planning will help. Business continuity planning has its greatest benefits in improving operational efficiency.

DISASTERS

A disaster is a very subjective concept so the use of the word within a continuity capability can lead to endless confusion and, worse, misunderstandings where one person thinks a disaster is covered and another does not. The worst problem with the use of 'disaster' is that it gives the impression that planning only needs to be done for these events and not for any other kind of outage. As a result no money should be allocated to the others. As has been noted some standards and a lot of the bodies of work on the subject of continuity planning imply that BCM is only for 'serious' events.

The word 'disaster' always connotes very dramatic events and tends to exclude non-dramatic events. So a building fire will usually be considered to be a 'disaster' whereas a breakdown of a single PC might not be, unless the PC happens to be running the entire shipping application suite.

A disaster can't be described in terms of drama or people. It is common to describe a disaster as a scenario where people have to move out of a building to another building and then back. Even more commonly it is now sometimes used to describe technical recovery or continuity and nothing else.

All of these are subjective and misleading. The only way to describe a disaster is in terms of business impact. The use of the word should be avoided in any event, because a 'disaster' is just another scenario involving a particular risk and should be treated in exactly the same way. The words 'disaster' and 'catastrophe' will not be used in this book, even though you will find liberal references to them in the standards bodies' work.

In the approach taken in this book, a disaster is simply another scenario. The scenario describes the event and a BCM procedure describes what should happen. Exactly the same approach is used as for a very simple failure, but the procedure could be more complex and would cover people as well, whereas some simple scenarios might just be 'break/fix'.

The advantage of this approach is that it removes confusion about what is important and once more ensures that the scenarios are understood by the people who will be involved. It is a lot easier to get support from a person or organisation when the question asked is, 'What would you do if the building was inaccessible due to fire?'

THE COST OF FAILURE

The big numbers usually used to describe the losses due to continuity failure tend to be over-dramatic so no-one believes that the consequences will be as bad as supposed. Actually they might believe them, but not when the next logical step is taken.This is to equate the loss with the investment justification. For example if the potential loss is 100 million pounds and the required investment is 2 million pounds, then this is justified. 'So can we have a budget of 2 million pounds?' 'No.'

The second issue here is that, for the overwhelming majority of risks, there is no relevant probability data. So even if the loss would be 100 million pounds of direct revenue and lost market share, what is the chance of the event happening? The usual result is for management to reverse the entire question by asking how much continuity protection they can get for a given investment and fitting the probability to make the equation balance. The result is something like, 'Yes, the loss would be 100 million pounds but the chances are so small that we won't bother to plan for that event'.

This approach simply does not work and ruins any credibility that an investment request might have. If this is required then tone down the numbers to something sensible and lay the emphasis on the positive – the cost of success.

THE COST OF SUCCESS

The key to financing BCM is to attempt to analyse the efficiency and cost savings from eliminating the small outages and pre-documenting things in general. This is a hard exercise but worth attempting. Every company, like almost every person, is badly prepared even for the expected, never mind the unexpected. Continuity is obtained by this type of planning despite the possibility of unexpected events.

As simple example suppose a printer breaks down and it takes 35 minutes to repair because the parts are not in stock, or the repair company cannot come, or the repair person is busy. (There could be many reasons but it takes 35 minutes to fix.) This printer was going to print the shipping tickets for a delivery lorry which is delayed by 35 minutes as a result. It is a delivery of steel and the lorry passes a weighbridge where the printer is located so the lorry cannot leave. If there had been some pre-planning, this could perhaps have been reduced to five minutes.

As a result the lorry is immobile for 30 minutes, as is the driver. The customer has also lost 30 minutes. Other work may have accumulated, so it needs to be delayed because the lorry is waiting on the weighbridge. The cumulative costs of a simple lack of planning are much higher than expected but this is not usually seen as a big business continuity problem. The question is, 'Why not?'

Suppose a company has many small breakdowns like this. The cost of fixing them is relatively small but the cumulative cost of the inefficiency and delay is potentially enormous. Fixing these small problems using a scenario-based process will fix the big problems too. Building typical breakdown scenarios using the people who know – in this case the lorry driver, since it has probably happened to him at least once before – is the way to build a continuity capability from ground level upwards, and to convince management to finance it without using the standard scare tactics.

With this approach business continuity is almost financed by stealth, since a lot of the actions needed are self-financing. Who would refuse to document a simple management process to order spare parts which had all the details needed and pre-planned? Such a document would be a simple BCM procedure for a type of failure but very often does not exist.

CUSTOMER SATISFACTION

When designing continuity solutions the only point of view that matters is that of the customer. As a result the chain of events leading to the customer is the key and not single components in that chain. As an example, how many banks have highly available/efficient/fault tolerant datacentres delivering retail banking to customers, but which run ATMs (automated teller machines) over bad communications lines to equipment with unstable operating systems? If I am a customer of this bank and the ATM doesn't work, telling me about the datacentre availability doesn't solve the problem for me. Bear this in mind when looking at continuity solutions.

Similarly customers are fairly tolerant of failure if it is handled correctly. Let's take the example of a plane and check-in at the airport. If customers arrive at an airport and their plane is late, a wise airline will provide full information regularly knowing that, even when it announces that the plane will be four hours late, this is better than providing no information at all. A ticket for a free meal goes a long way towards keeping customers happy even though the objective service level is intolerable. The same applies to any business.

Hence any continuity solution should look at the entire chain of events with customer satisfaction in mind and a fairly high emphasis on customer communications. Communications should be part of every continuity procedure and it makes sense to share the responsibility between the person writing the procedure and a person whose specific job it is to communicate to customers. This is unlikely to be the Communications function because there is always a sales angle to dealing with customers. Who likes anonymous communications with no human contact? Alternatively, if there is a service desk function, then train people in this function on how to handle customers 'off script' (i.e. without simply following the types of script used to deal with incidents).

SOME INDUSTRIES ARE DIFFERENT

They are not; at least they should not follow different processes. Any differences arise from the definition of a 'line of business'. In other words at what level of granularity is business reported and managed so that a reasoned judgment can be made as to which lines of business must be of higher priority than others when it comes to continuity decisions?

Some businesses only have a single line of business. This makes life easier since there are no decisions to be made when it comes to priorities. With multiple lines of business the problem is more complex and, in reality, it is rare for a line of business to be abandoned when there is a continuity problem. It can happen: for example, in a logistics business, email on the move may be dropped or, in a white goods factory, spares production could be dropped short-term.

However the most common problem arises when there are support functions which behave like lines of business rather than cost centres. If the support function really has revenue, margin and cost targets, then it is, for all intents and purposes, a line of business and should be treated as such. If its 'revenue' is shadow revenue then this doesn't count and the support function is a resource only. IT is most often a resource for business which may govern itself by, for example, cost recovery targets but this does not make it a business in the terms defined here.

When looking at lines of business, make sure the revenue is real revenue and avoid the mistake of counting losses of revenue by your customers as a justification for investment in continuity. If the customer is prepared to pay for you to have continuity plans to cover risks which are specific to the customer then this is acceptable. If not, the risks and potential revenue losses belong to the customer and not you and your plans and investments should only cover your potential losses.

2 IN PRACTICE – THE FOUNDATIONS

In general keep horizons short and deliverables at stages where management can see them and their value. However there is some groundwork to do if a project is to be successful. These are all critical success factors when the project is going to take a long time to complete.

Defining the strategy and policy (below) are gating factors. If these do not exist the project has no foundation and stakeholders will always have a very good reason not to cooperate. Unless they are in place the project should not start. If the strategy exists in a non-formal way then drive to get it documented in such a way that, explicitly or implicitly, business continuity is included.

COMPANY STRATEGY

The first thing a company has to define is its **strategy**. This is a statement of strategic intent which defines the position of a business in the face of competitive issues in the broadest sense. For example a company may say, 'Our strategy is to become the leader in the generic drug segment,' or, 'Part of our strategy is to ensure that our customers enjoy better service levels than they will find in competitive product offerings'.

Very often strategy is placed after policy in BCM planning and is a statement of how things will be done. This is a mistake as policy is an implementation tool for the overall strategy. Once the strategic intent is defined then policy initially states who is affected, the expected performance and the way compliance to these standards will be measured.

Do not be surprised if the overall company strategy does not go down to the level of including business continuity. There should be some statement in the company strategy which supports BCM. Any reference to customer service or to the market being addressed will generally provide support for BCM. In the two examples above continuity is one of the components needed to provide good customer service, and being a market leader usually requires conformance to regulatory requirements (including continuity) and alignment with market trends (which include continuity).

In any event, write a BCM Strategy document that simply shows how BCM helps to implement the strategy but without going into details. There is an example below.

CONTINUITY STRATEGY

There are two rather conflicting definitions from BS25999 part 2:

> *The approach by an organization that will ensure its recovery and continuity in the face of a disaster or other major incident or business disruption*

and

> *...to identify BCM arrangements that will enable the organization to recover its critical activities within their recovery time objectives*

The first issue with this is that the definition talks about disasters and major incidents – this is only part of a business continuity capability. Second, business continuity is not solely focused on recovering within recovery time objectives, but should focus also on the recovery of business to acceptable service levels within acceptable times with a service level which could be lower than normal.

So what should a strategy document be used for and define? A BCM Strategy defines the business position on the subject of continuity. A broader strategic statement will cover other aspects of a business as above. Some good strategic statements for a BCM Strategy are:

- Business levels will be restored after an outage to levels which are acceptable only.
- Alternative sites will always be prepared, being the first mechanism to restore business – swapover will occur after any outage whilst original site recovery proceeds.
- Manual service will always be provided when IT breaks down.
- Contingency plans for delivery will be established (if alternative means of transport are needed during outages).

The point here is that these statements are an expression of strategic intent and show how things will be done. They define the framework of business continuity. With these statements you can go to the shipping manager, for example, and request an alternative shipping plan. Without such a document, or with only a policy document, he could refuse.

Similarly you can go to other managers to ask for their manual alternative service plans; to the IT and Facilities management teams to ask for their plans to move work to alternative sites; and to the accountants to ask for the money for the alternative sites.

Clearly it is not quite as simple as this and these plans will be produced with the help of the BCM implementation team rather than the individuals themselves, but the point is that the strategy document enables you to move into action.

Strategy documents are only of any use if the statements can be made into concrete plans afterwards. A good way to look at strategic statements is to equate them with action plans and people who will be responsible for those plans like this:

Table 1.1 Strategic statements and action plans

Strategic statement	Action	Who
Delivery of goods will use alternative means of transport during outages	• Define alternative transport plan	• Transport manager
Customer delivery will take priority	• Communicate to clients as soon as an outage occurs • Prioritise shipments • Restore shipping application as first priority	• Customer representative • Transport manager • IT manager

As can be seen, the strategy statements can result in multiple actions for multiple managers and expressing the statements in this way provides a good basis for communication and influence with management. This should form a part of the overall plan of influencing stakeholders to do what is needed to implement BCM. It also has the advantage that stakeholders can see what others are doing as well.

BUSINESS CONTINUITY POLICY

A policy is by definition a simple, fairly short (i.e. short enough for people to bother to read it) document that is addressed to everyone in the business and defines who is affected. All too often policies are long-winded documents which partially cover strategy and options and sometimes even implementation. Often they are addressed to everyone but circulated or made available only to a limited number of people, and often they use language which makes some stakeholders feel it does not apply to them.

A policy should also explain who it applies to in a level of detail that is sufficient for people to feel included, empowered and responsible. Hence it is also relevant to include some words on how it will be implemented and measured. After reading a policy document a stakeholder should know what has to be done, how it applies to the stakeholder and why. Keep it simple – there is no shame in writing documents which are short.

A policy should include the following types of statement:

Statement of intent or BCM Policy Statement: Business continuity and our ability to demonstrate it is required by regulation, our customers and our competitive position.

Statement of inclusion: This policy applies to all departments, business units and functions, and to all staff within those areas. There are no exceptions.

Statement of seriousness: The policy will be applied and audit will occur yearly. Failure of audit could be grounds for dismissal (this is **really** serious).

Statement of the policy details: All business units, departments and functions must be able to show that they have undertaken a Business Impact Analysis for their areas, assessed the risks to their areas and developed business continuity plans which have been implemented and tested on a regular basis. Business continuity plans must be accurate and fully documented, and able to handle all of the incident scenarios identified in the risk analysis. All departments, business units and functions must assign a business continuity coordinator who will be responsible for managing outages according to the plan. There will be a central committee to coordinate all actions in the event of outages and handle escalations.

Statement of compliance: Compliance will be measured by internal audit yearly against the objectives and measures defined in the Business Continuity Governance framework.

Simple – everyone is included, they have no choice and the bare bones of what the policy requires are highlighted. Make it longer where necessary but unambiguous. Having such a document makes the management and implementation of BCM easier. No manager can now say he does not have the time, resources or will to do this. It has to be done. It could include a statement of when it has to be implemented. Since the policy is a tool which forms part of the implementation of the strategy, objections should be easy to handle since they would be fundamentally questioning the *raison d'être* of the business.

PLANNING

Regardless of the level of executive sponsorship or budget assigned to the BCM project, the commitment will fade over time and BCM projects are notorious for the time they take. Getting the strategic statement and policy in place first is important and the governance should be discussed with all stakeholders prior to any project planning. People will react better to plans if they know in advance why they are being created and what is going to be expected of them.

Project planning serves two purposes: it helps a team plan work over an extended period and keeps them on track but, more important, it is the tool by which management stakeholders are influenced. Doing the planning without their commitment is a big mistake.

The first action before doing any detailed planning is to present an abbreviated plan to stakeholders to ensure they agree. **No** detailed planning should be done at this stage because it is impossible to know what the stakeholders are going to say to the high-level plan.

For example the high-level plan could propose a milestone date which is too late for some stakeholders or unrealistically early for others. Until the date is understood and agreed, planning in detail cannot start. This sounds elementary but it is surprising how many project managers start from a stakeholder agreement to run a project, then start to plan in detail, then start the project using their detailed plan and then find out six months later that their milestone dates are not acceptable. Do not assume that a commitment to run a project means that everyone knows what will then happen. And yes, it is possible to get an acceptable idea of milestone dates without doing all the detailed planning. The results will not be 100% accurate but they never are anyway.

3   BUSINESS IMPACT ANALYSIS

INTRODUCTION

The Business Impact Analysis (BIA) is the key tool in the development of BCM plans. There are key objectives in doing a BIA and these should be borne in mind during the process to avoid wasted effort:

- A BIA raises management attention as to what is important and what is not. Received opinion will be that everything is important, especially if the person asked has a vested interest. It would be hard to get an objective opinion of, for example, the importance of payroll by asking the person who runs it. In this obvious example payroll can fail for a couple of months if the continuity plan is to pay people what they received in the last month before the failure.

- A BIA highlights which resources (people, plant, IT etc.) are important. The resources used for individual parts of a business are rarely well-documented and frequently limited to a restricted view. Is a building important and, if so, are there alternatives? Are people important and, if so, are their skills replaceable? Having a full map of the resources for critical parts of a business allows proper planning.

- A BIA determines which parts of the business are of priority in the short term. Not all parts of a business are important and criticality should be determined by revenue and profit. Not all parts of a business need to recover immediately and the BIA should focus on prioritisation based on financial issues alone. Full analysis below a certain threshold is a waste of effort. Revenue should be viewed in the broadest sense – it is not just direct revenue from sales but also deferred revenue and what could be called 'intangible revenue' (loss of market share and reputation for example).

- A BIA provides the opportunity for all stakeholders to look at the threats to a business and come to a common understanding of which will produce real risks that need to be mitigated or accepted. It is very common for different parts of a business to have very different ideas of risk and do very different things about those risks (often wasting resources in the process). For example, with a limited amount to spend on mitigating risk, is it better to take out transport insurance or to build a second datacentre for disaster recovery?

There are no other good reasons for doing a BIA.

Without a BIA it is impossible to know whether the money spent on mitigation efforts is too much or too little. Without a BIA negotiating with any shareholder becomes a question of opinion rather than fact and this generally means that getting money to do anything is rendered very difficult. A BIA also serves to focus the mind. Many stakeholders will have an opinion but a BIA formalises these opinions and forces people to choose. This formalisation and documentation serves a useful purpose in itself.

Impact analysis is difficult for a number of reasons. The major one is that most stakeholders will have very little idea of the real impact in term of revenue without going into the more complex issues of deferred or potential revenue (for example reputational risk). Similarly risk appetite sounds good but, when it comes down to defining or deciding upon the level of risk, stakeholders prefer not to choose.

BIA is also dogged by detail. Many people want to analyse to a level of detail which misses the object of the exercise – to prioritise. It is very easy to criticise any BIA by claiming that it does not have the details but it is important to remember that there is a cut-off point. The major culprit in this area is doing a BIA at the application level, which is almost always a level of detail too far.

However by avoiding these mistakes the BIA is a very useful tool and a simple exercise. Indeed the simpler it is the more chance it has of gaining support from management.

One thing to remember is that the results of a BIA will always be qualitative, so searching for quantitative results is a waste of time and money. Additionally a BIA will always be wrong in some level of detail and at some time in the future: like most parts of BCM a BIA is something to be kept up-to-date, rather than being a definitive, objective, quantitative exercise.

THE OBJECTIVES OF THE BIA

In general terms these high-level objectives are to be met:

- gaining broad agreement from business management as to the potential losses of critical business components;
- gaining agreement on the threats to the business;
- gaining agreement on the maximum tolerable outages for each line of business;
- proposing broad risk reduction and mitigation steps;
- focusing risk mitigation and analysis on critical areas, as opposed to all areas of a business (as is often the case);

- starting to get a preliminary idea of the order of magnitude of the investments needed to minimise the potential revenue loss. This covers losses of tangible revenue as well as those due to intangibles such as reputation.

LEVEL OF DETAIL AND SCOPE

The BIA is what its name implies – a business level analysis. There are countless plans which are conceived by looking at IT alone or, worse, by looking at applications and analysing interdependencies. These common approaches are not merely wrong, but negligent.

The correct, indeed only, approach is to look at a business from a business point of view. The 'application' approach fails for a simple reason – no business or part of a business depends only upon either a single application or a group of applications. All the resources used to realise the revenue associated with the group of applications are in scope when it comes to looking at the impact of losing this revenue stream. The IT approach fails for the same reason. Any break in the chain causes a problem and the business is defined by these chains of events, not only by the IT part. Indeed any approach which does not look at the whole chain of events used in generating current and future revenue will lead to false results. We can use this as a definition of a line of business (LOB) in fact.

In some businesses the number of lines of business is very low. It could be that the business is a single business line which does one thing and has a monolithic accounting system for this and a single management team. This is perfectly reasonable and does not invalidate the approach.

An example of this could be an internet-only electronics outlet. It sells a variety of products to retail customers and takes credit cards in payment. All delivery is handled by the local postal service. This business happens to have multiple product lines and accounts for them by product group, with each product group having a different product group manager.

When we do a Business Impact Analysis on this company the picture starts to change. Product group A has a group of customers who are ready to accept longer delivery times than product group B. This means that the impact on B will be higher than A since A has a longer maximum tolerable outage (MTO). Product group C is low-turnover and low-risk.

Table 3.1 MTOs and daily revenues for product groups

Product group	MTO	Revenue per day	Resources needed
A = LCD TVs	5 days	£100,000	Order entry systems, stock systems, network, high warehouse space, postal service, Supplier A
B = Memory chips	1 day	£25,000	Order entry systems, stock systems, network, low warehouse space, postal service, Supplier B
C = Motherboards	3 days	£5,000	Order entry systems, network

In this example the three product groups share almost all the same resources since the business is monolithic. The differences are only in the suppliers and amounts of warehouse space they use. In the case of product group C the product is ordered and shipped directly from the supplier to the customer, so the only things needed are an ordering system and a network.

In this business the most critical business is product line B – it has the highest revenue per day and the lowest MTO. When looking at the risks to the resources needed, mitigation will have some impact on the other product lines as well, but the approach should be to look at the product line first and the resources second. In other words don't try to fix the common resources because they affect other lines of business as well. This will draw the focus away from what matters (product line B) and make the exercise unnecessarily cumbersome.

CRITICAL SUCCESS FACTORS

A BIA takes time and effort and is often viewed as a useless exercise by management with other work to do and a restricted view of the total business. The following are critical factors:

- **Senior management support**: Not as a sponsor only but as a body that wants reports and is accountable for the results, which is paying for it to be done and which will provide real support when staff cooperation is not forthcoming.

- **Time**: It takes a few months to do properly and to come up with results which can be acted upon, and which all parties agree to. It will take almost as long to prepare and present the data as to gather it.

- **A team**: This is not a one-man exercise. Many people will need to be interviewed and the result has to be a common agreement. Get the major management stakeholders together to discuss how it will be done, and share results early and often.

- **A single project manager.**

Before starting a BIA exercise the BCM project manager needs to be sure these four items are known and agreed. This forms part of the communication but these items are called critical success factors for a reason. As with other forms of communication this is not a one-way exercise – it requires a positive agreement rather than a passive one. That management come to a presentation and do not disagree represents passive agreement (in other words no agreement).

Remember too that without a BIA it is impossible to know if the amount of money that could be spent on mitigation is too high or low. As a result it is impossible for someone to justifiably say that a solution is too expensive. Since the BIA is going to lead directly to a budget at some point, the budget cannot be known until the BIA is done. Note that there is a difference between the budget allocated and the amount that could be spent – the budget is always lower, which represents the risk appetite and acceptance of risks.

ASSESSING IMPACT

For this first step of a BIA we should concentrate on the impact if a line of business either stops or no longer works at full capacity. This only applies to scenarios where the outage is longer than the MTO.

There are two ways that can be used to assess the impact, bearing in mind that this assessment is done to determine what continuity planning or other mitigation actions should be put in place and what budget assigned. Do not expect the BIA to give anything more than a prioritisation. In fact do not run a BIA with any other intention, otherwise you will drown in irrelevant details.

The two methods are qualitative and quantitative – qualitative means the results are a judgment only and quantitative means there is objective data available. In a BIA the data on direct revenue is normally quantitative – look in the accounts or ask the accountants and they can tell you the numbers. This is probably the only source of quantitative data in this whole exercise – when we look at the subject of risk later, it can be clearly assumed that no quantitative data exists.

If you want the data on the revenue losses over time the question is more complex:

- Would **all** of the revenue be lost if the product or service were not supplied?
- Would customers come back after an outage?
- After what length of time would revenue losses start?

Quantitative
The BIA questionnaires are used to gather this data. When an outage occurs an LOB manager will be able to state the extent of these and when they will start.

This is sufficient for a BIA. The manager may not be able to assess those losses which are not related to direct revenue (such as reputation loss, market share loss etc.) so the only method here is to assess these qualitatively. The same table as for risk should be used.

Qualitative
Use this scheme when completing the impact section of the BIA questionnaire.

- **Very Low**: Minimal business impact.
- **Low**: Some business impact but any issues can be handled without long-term effects on customers, delivery or service.
- **Medium**: Business impact is significant, which will cause extra work to recover.
- **High**: High business impact which will cause work, customer dissatisfaction, loss of customers potentially.
- **Very High**: Very high business impact which will threaten the survival of the business.

REVENUE AT RISK

One technique which will help decision making is the concept of 'revenue at risk'. As an example, if a business outage causes revenue to stop after one month, the revenue per month is £1 million and business recovery takes two months, we could say that the revenue at risk is £2 million. If we can avoid this by some mitigation action of cost X the result is easy to digest – X spent has an effective return of £2 million.

It is never this simple! The revenue in this example ignores the potential future losses of revenue because of lost market share or dissatisfied customers and any regulatory penalties (for some businesses). It also glosses over the fact that it is rare that a single action will prevent an event. The truth is more complex even though the theory is the same.

Table 3.2 Calculating revenue losses

Business line	MTO	Revenue loss after 24 hours (£)	Revenue loss after 48 hours (£)	Revenue loss after one week (£)
A	4 hours	500	1,000	3,500
B	48 hours	0	0	1,000
C	30 minutes	1,000	10,000	20,000
Cumulative		1,500	12,500	37,000

Business A is fairly linear – it produces £500 per day. Business B is fairly tolerant of failure and can function for 48 hours without loss. Business C is intolerant – losses start immediately and increase over time.

If need be we could now plot this to provide a graphic illustration of the cumulative totals. This provides an easy view of where risk appetite could be located. However simply gathering this type of data and presenting it to all stakeholders in this tabular form is a useful eye-opening exercise in itself.

QUESTIONNAIRES

Business Impact Analysis
There is a simplified BIA questionnaire in the Templates section which can be used to gather the majority of the information needed. It should be prepared and sent in advance to allow time for answers to be considered. It must not be a substitute for an interview. The line of business owner is the person with the financial responsibility for this area. It is realistic, but not advisable, that the person who will complete the questionnaire will be a member of staff rather than the business owner. However for the interview process and the final agreed and signed document it is critical that the business owner takes the responsibility.

Functional department threats/risks
This template is used to interview supporting functions rather than business functions. There is no hard and fast rule as to who this will be but, typically, Facilities and IT are supporting functions which have major roles in underpinning any company. If the business is delivery the transport function will be managed separately and play a key and broad role, so they should be interviewed using this. The people interviewed using this questionnaire do not usually have a revenue generation role *per se* but provide most of the service to business management.

Examples of typical supporting functions by industry are these although this is not an exhaustive list. Each business is different so only a proper analysis of the business prior to the BIA will show which functions generate revenue and which provide support:

Table 3.3 Supporting functions

Industry	Supporting functions
Any (applies to all industries)	IT function, Facilities
Logistics	Transport, customer facing representatives, service desk
Manufacturing	Production line, transport

Functional departments clearly play a crucial role in the continuity plans of any business, since lines of business rely upon them and usually have no alternative. This does not alter the need for a BIA, since there is often a need to make a choice between the continuity capabilities of multiple lines of business.

The intention here is to get the point of view of people who are not business owners but who have vast experience of how a business runs. These stakeholders will have a very practical view about what really represents a threat and what are the risks that occur in practice. Not having their input, and relying solely upon the view of LOB management, will give a restricted view and may result in spending too little or too much. Functional departments like these will also provide a very practical view of what mitigations are already, or could be, in place, since part of the process of a BIA is to propose broad mitigations of risk.

This does not mean that all that needs to be done is to ensure the ability of the functional departments. This assumption leads to continuity plans which focus heavily, and sometimes solely, on a single department like IT or Facilities. This approach then leads to plans which only cover part of the chain. A good example would be analysing a line of business at the application level within IT and then looking for the interdependencies: not only is this a level of detail too far but it misses the people and resource scenarios which are often the major causes of failure.

TOOLS

For practical purposes you will find all you need with the standard Microsoft Office suite. Tools in the right hands can be useful but be sure to make the choice based on the objectives – documenting what you do is the first, tracking is the second and updating is the third. If the tool can do these without them becoming major jobs then it is fit for purpose.

The major problem with a business continuity tool of any description is that it can overtake common sense, and the original objectives can get lost in a perceived need to use it. Worse, the use of the tool becomes the objective and it is assumed that, if the tool is used and completed, the plan is implemented. Wrong.

A lot of tools automate the tracking of when impact analyses need to be updated or risks need to be reviewed. The danger here is that, if you need a tool to automate this, the chances are that the work is too complicated and, if this is the case, the continuity capability probably won't work. Remember that we should only be tracking a limited number of risks – since some are accepted – and a limited number of scenarios, and that continuity will be applied only to those parts of the business where the impact of loss is unacceptable. The responsibility to know when new risks to a line of business arise lies clearly and simply with the LOB manager, rather than with the tool or the BCM project office. Given this the use of any tracking tool needs careful review, so that it does not become an end in itself.

Once BCM procedures are designed and tested there will be a need for online and offline copies to be available and some tools can help here. Once more, though, the watchword should be 'simplicity'. Stakeholders really need a copy of the BCM procedures with all the contact data and the procedure to follow when something goes wrong. Any other information is cosmetic.

THE PROCESS IN DETAIL

It is usually easier to split the impact analysis from the risk analysis, which will be dealt with in the next section. In practice the steps can be summarised as follows:

(i)   Project kick off and definition of scope of the BIA:

- Define which part of the business is to be considered. Typically this will be a division or service. When it is agreed it is important that the impact to this part of the company alone is considered. The impact must be something that the business managers interviewed can control. For example if a business manager provides a service to someone and the service user can lose money but the service provider cannot, this is irrelevant for the purposes of the BIA. The exact scope must be made clear at the start of the process.

(ii) Preparation and distribution of BIA and threat questionnaires:

- A questionnaire is prepared and sent in advance. This is simply to give time for answers to be considered. It must not be a substitute for an interview. The business owner is the person with the financial responsibility for this area. It is realistic, but not advisable, that the person who will complete the questionnaire will be a member of staff rather than the business owner. However for the interview process and the final agreed and signed document it is critical that the business owner takes the responsibility.

(iii) Interviews with business management:

- Questionnaires are distributed in advance and interviews take place at least a week later. Preparing answers in advance is important but the interview process gathers more subjective information. The questionnaires are designed around open questions. The questions don't give pre-defined values – such as Low/Medium/High – since these can be too easy to complete and can hide the truth. It is better is ask an open question and **listen**.

- Remember that the subject of this exercise is **their** business and what you are doing is to help **them**. All too often these interviews can take place in a strained atmosphere because the value is not seen.

- It will be immediately evident that managers think their businesses are important. In reality it may turn out that this is not the case, or at least that their businesses might be low on the priority list. The interviewer should express no opinion on this.

(iv)   Review of results and re-interviews (if necessary):

- After consolidation of results there may be a need to clarify certain points, particularly with regard to financial business impact. This clarification can be done by phone, mail or re-interview. It is important to remember that all the data gathered is **subjective**. By definition there is no objective truth and the final results will not be precise. Re-interviewing to gain precise information is a waste of their and your time and is unnecessary. As a rule of thumb if revenue figures are accurate to 10–15% this is fine. This is sufficiently accurate for all areas in general.

(v)   Interviews with functional management around threats:

- The interviews may be longer and the data is often more accurate. Particular emphasis should be put on the historical information regarding outages, since this is a mine of information for the future. Use the questionnaire.

(vi)   Consolidation and review of results.

(vii)   Report preparation and presentation.

Maximum Tolerable Outage (MTO)

Analysing the potential business losses you would experience depending on the period of disruption of the service (for example one hour, four hours etc.) will allow the management to come to an agreed figure for MTO. There are no standards here and the figure agreed can and will vary from person to person.

When doing a BIA for a business where the scope covers many lines of business, expect variable results and then either report them all separately or try to agree on a consolidated figure. Remember that the key purpose of this figure is to enable you to decide what to do in scenarios where the outage time exceeds the MTO and it can be that there aren't any! This is entirely dependent upon the business and the appetite for risk, since it may be that the MTO is low but management simply decide they will take the risk of any outage exceeding this. This is entirely subjective.

Similarly an MTO could be judged as two hours but, when scenarios are developed and procedures written and tested, the actual capability is four. At first glance this would seem to imply that the MTO should be four hours too. However nothing stops management taking the risk that these scenarios won't happen and ignoring the four hour reality.

4   THE BUSINESS IMPACT ANALYSIS REPORT

Before going any further a report has to be written to inform all stakeholders of the results of the BIA and gain agreement to continue and on a budget for doing so. This report will cover the impact to the lines of business in scope, the threats perceived, the risks retained and the current and future mitigations proposed.

It is a very sensitive document and one thing to bear in mind when interviewing people is to assure them that nothing in a final report will be nominative so they can speak freely. It is also very important to avoid exaggeration of losses and remain factual, since the objective is to gain agreement and resources to proceed further. You will see both extremes: LOB managers who do not see the impact to their businesses and others who think the entire enterprise relies on their businesses alone.

When such a report is presented it will be interpreted according to the current politics rather than the logic you think you have expressed, so it will need considerable review with the project sponsor before being presented. Note that presentation is more important than circulation to stakeholders. Circulated documents never get read.

Remember that, if the BIA is being done now, it is likely that problems have been uncovered. It may be that business does not know what is actually being spent on risk mitigation or, worse, that money is being spent on parts of the business that are simply not critical to revenue generation. A good example here is Procurement – it is very unlikely that the loss of this service will affect short-term revenue and that there are not simple workarounds. Similarly the state of readiness may be much worse than expected and this is sensitive information.

Bearing this in mind here are some suggestions as to the content and ways to present results:

- Describe the background to the project. Why was it started? Who started it? What is the organisation's structure in brief and who are the sponsors. What is the exact scope?

- Executive summary. During a BIA there will be observations made to reduce threats and risk and improve resilience in the face of impact etc. These may apply to cross-business unit functions (such as Facilities), individual business units or even business processes and applications. The executive summary should provide a quick overview of these recommendations as well as an overview of the current potential impact and the business units that this would affect.

- Describe the deliverables in terms of workshops, presentations, reports and questionnaires. Define the content of the final report in some detail to ensure that both parties know what information is being sought.

- Describe the methodology used and who was interviewed (by function not name).

- Describe the timelines up to the current stage with a rough projection for the future (assuming the project proceeds).

- For each business area describe the results in terms of impact as a simple High/Medium/Low with comments.

- Describe threats and weaknesses via a heatmap. The intention is simply to highlight which future projects could reduce threat levels and risk exposure, regardless of whether full-scale business continuity planning proceeds.

Figure 4.1 Heatmap comparing frequency and impact of threats

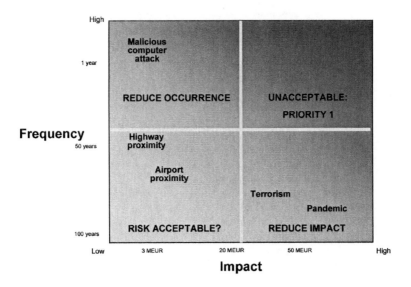

- For each interviewee there are questions on readiness. The degree of preparation for outage directly affects potential losses. There could be

business areas of high potential impact but which have a high readiness, so the overall impact that they would suffer would be low. The inverse can be true as well. A heatmap is also a good way to show this by plotting business areas against readiness, as in this example:

• A simple map of which resources are critical for each business. This focuses attention on these and will connect to the risk analysis later, since priority should be given to those business areas where the critical resources run risks. **Everything about a BIA report is to focus and prioritise based on impact**.

Figure 4.2 Heatmap comparing impact of events with preparation

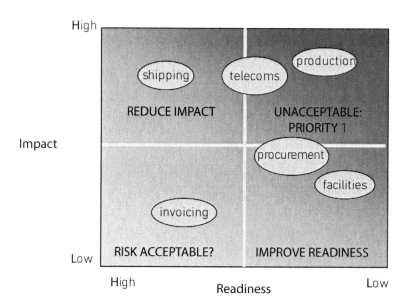

• Revenue loss projections. Another convenient way to show impact is to show when revenue would start to be lost. This is done by plotting the standard revenue stream on a graph and, next to it, the revenue decline after each point when it begins to dip due to a previous event. The difference is the revenue loss projection. This helps you to understand where investment should occur.

Figure 4.3 Revenue loss projection

Revenue at risk

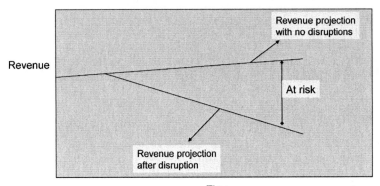

* Recovery time and point objectives as perceived by business managers. In cases where some of these appear unrealistic, there is some fairly objective data on market statistics at the end which may help. It is very common for business managers to have completely unrealistic ideas of what they are capable of providing and what their customers want or would tolerate. However the delicate part here is that, until scenarios are developed and procedures defined and tested, there is nothing other than a subjective view of real capability. So use market statistics to raise the point. It is also easier to simply discuss recovery times at this stage rather than introducing recovery point objectives.

5 THREATS, RISKS AND RISK ANALYSIS

There is a lot of confusion in the terminology used in this domain so, for the purposes of this book, these are the terms that will be used:

Threats: Areas or things that can go wrong without regard to their probability or impact. For example 'plague of locusts'.

Risks: Things that can go wrong but combined with some idea of the chances of them happening and how much impact they would have. The risk of a plague of locusts is small because it has very low probability and the impact is judged to be low.

Threat analysis: Looking at those areas where things can go wrong. This is often called risk analysis but this is too confusing when there is also a definition of risk assessment.

Risk assessment: Analysing probabilities and effects and deciding what to do – accept, reduce or plan.

INTRODUCTION

Threat analysis and risk assessment is a secondary exercise. You don't look for risks in areas where the business impact is low. Use the BIA results to eliminate those areas of low business impact before you start.

The theory of risk is at odds with the way people view it or deal with it. If you ask someone what a risk is the example answer will usually be of the form, 'This item breaks down'. This is not a risk, in theory, since it should be expressed as an effect and a probability. People don't think this way in general so why force them to? When it comes to probabilities the best that people can manage is usually high or low (sometimes medium). Since this is the way people think it is best to go along with it, rather than try (in vain) to make it align to theory. When it comes to probabilities there is simply no data. Actuarial data is the result of very long histories of slow-moving events and, by definition, modern business moves more quickly, so it is arguable that no historical data applies to current events. Worse, actuarial data might be reasonably good for things like car insurance, but can it tell you how often a disc will break down or a fire will break out?

First some standard definitions. If a risk analysis is to be done according to the book – and some people may ask you to do this – then it is worth knowing the book terminology.

RISK ANALYSIS:

The systematic process to understand the nature of, and to deduce the level of risk.

- Provides the basis for risk evaluation and decisions about risk treatment.

AS/NZS 4360:2004

Systematic use of information to identify sources and to estimate the risk.

- Risk analysis provides a basis for risk evaluation, risk treatment and risk acceptance.
- Information can include historical data, theoretical analysis, informed opinions and the concerns of stakeholders.

ISO/IEC GUIDE 73:2002

Systematic use of available information to identify hazards and to estimate the risk.

ISO/IEC Guide 51:1999

Risk analysis is a technique to identify and assess factors that may jeopardize the success of a project or achieving a goal. This technique also helps to define preventive measures to reduce the probability of these factors from occurring and identify countermeasures to successfully deal with these constraints when they develop to avert possible negative effects on the competitiveness of the company.

Wikipedia

IN PRACTICE

You should look at a business and **analyse** the areas or things that could go wrong – the '**threats**' in the terminology used here. You should then do some more in-depth **assessment** to work out the chances of these happening and the impact that they would have – the **risks**. Why there are so many definitions is a mystery.

During the assessment process there are two pieces of information which are needed. The first is the impact when something happens and the second the probability of its happening.

RISK ASSESSMENT:

The overall process of risk identification, risk analysis and risk evaluation.

AS/NZS 4360:2004

Overall process of risk analysis and risk evaluation.

ISO/IEC GUIDE 73:2002

Overall process comprising a risk analysis and a risk evaluation.

ISO/IEC Guide 51:1999

Risk assessment is a step in a risk management process. Risk assessment is the determination of quantitative or qualitative value of risk related to a concrete situation and a recognized threat (also called hazard). Quantitative risk assessment requires calculations of two components of risk: R, the magnitude of the potential loss L, and the probability p, that the loss will occur.

Wikipedia

Here is an example. After analysing threat areas we find that people agree that a big threat is a fire in a warehouse where we keep some stock for shipment. Everyone agrees this is a threat area even though we have fire drills and extinguishers and the building is built to good standards. However we cannot agree on the impact or the chances of its happening. To avoid endless discussion (i.e. wasting money) and arguments about whose source of data is right, and circumvent the fact that there is no sound actuarial data covering most risks anyway, we adopt a quantitative method where the people trying to solve this problem can find some common ground. In general there are a couple of tables used.

The first covers the impact, since coming to a financial number is well-nigh impossible in most cases and the object of the exercise is to prioritise so the biggest numbers count, not their absolute values. The second table would be one covering probabilities, expressed as either quantitative values or a translation of these into either a scoring system or a percentage. In any event the actual values are not especially relevant, since they are ultimately used to prioritise which risks are dealt with. There is always a cut-off point since dealing with all risks is not cost-effective or practical. Both tables are in this section.

RISK LIFECYCLE

Below is the recommended cycle of events:

Figure 5.1 Lifecycle of risk analysis and management

The above cycle works on a regular basis. Once per year or every two years should suffice. Some regulations say or imply that this should be yearly but the more common view, and one which an auditor would like to see, is that the risk exercise is done at least every two years or when there are major changes in perceived threats.

The steps are these:

Review threats with stakeholders to agree risk areas

Go through an exercise with stakeholders and, in particular, the functional departments to agree which areas of threat represent areas of risk. Using the threat database helps to generate input if there is none or if a stakeholder thinks there is no risk in a particular area. The threat database is generic but the exercise can go to further levels of detail. It really does not matter if this covers all threats since this exercise will be repeated and there is ample opportunity, even during plan development, to introduce new scenarios to align with risks which have been overlooked in the beginning.

Using a threat database to provoke discussion gains a lot of support because it is easy. Most risk analysis and assessment exercises fail because they produce too much data and generally use dubious mathematics to produce reports that no-one believes as a result. One of the unintended consequences is that the exercise takes such a long time that support is lost, yet risk analysis only benefits the company in the long term if it is a regular exercise driven by stakeholders.

Here is a list of broad threat areas that can affect a business. The level of detail here is relatively low since we are seeking the interviewee's ideas and opinions on what can affect his business or the asset he controls which supports a business:

Process failure: Caused by faulty design, inadequate process – control, inadequately documented processes or simply people not following the prescribed processes. Are roles and responsibilities in recovering from crises defined, published and known?

Operational failures: Things that can go wrong but are not caused by malice. For example running the wrong programmes, forgetting to do backups, overwriting data etc.

Technical failure: Failure of technical components such as hardware, systems or networks (telecoms included).

Human failure: Caused by human factors in general.

Logical failure: Application errors or errors due to development and design faults.

Natural disaster: Examples include epidemics, floods, fire and earthquakes.

Failure of subcontractors of any type: Examples are utilities (gas, water, electrical power, resources, material, services, partners generally). Includes any external services the business might use.

Sabotage: Deliberate acts of any kind, whether caused by employees or external parties.

This can be used as a broad introduction. Threats should be assessed by interviews either individually or in groups. It is likely that the first opinions of threats will be fairly vague, in which case the spreadsheet below should be used to provoke thought. Use the threats in it to question whether the interviewees see them as areas where things have happened in the past and, if so, use them as the starting point for developing typical scenarios.

Remember that the key to success here is making sure that the threats/risks are seen and understood by the participants and not seen as part of some theoretical exercise. For each threat they identify they are going to come up with a scenario and then write a procedure to handle it. This is potentially a lot of work initially so it is important that a sense of ownership be encouraged from the beginning. This is more easily done if they identify the threats themselves. The key here is the participation of stakeholders.

Discard some threat areas and retain those agreed
There will be threats which are considered unimportant. Discard these so that the next step concentrates only on the ones people agree upon.

Risk assessment with stakeholders
For the retained threats, convert these into risks by looking at the impact of each and the probability of its occurring. Use impact and probability tables as below.

Impact
Impact table method 1

Very Low: Minimal business impact. Score = 1.

Low: Some business impact but any issues can be handled without long-term effects on customers, delivery or service (2).

Medium: Business impact is significant and recovery will cause extra work (3).

High: High business impact which will cause further work, customer dissatisfaction and potentially loss of customers (4).

Very High: Very high business impact which will threaten the survival of the business (5).

Impact table method 2

30 days – Deferrable: Recovery can be delayed because it is not absolutely necessary for the normal business to function. Loss has little or no impact on the organisation (for example information/historical files). Score = 1.

5 days – Important: The loss allows the business function to continue but not as smoothly as it otherwise would (2).

3 days – Necessary: This business function is needed to operate smoothly. The function is necessary to maintain control of the organisation. Time and volume are key factors. The function could become Critical to Vital if lost for a prolonged period. The function is normally needed to support business and management decisions (4).

24 hours – Critical: The business suffers a severe impact if this function is not available (7).

8 hours – Vital: The business cannot perform meaningful work without this function. The function is mission critical and absolutely essential for the organisation to remain operational (10).

When evaluating the impact of loss or interruption the valuation should be done covering all the potential losses. Very often the direct loss of revenue is a lower one than that of customers and reputation.

Using a combination of the above tables a group of people can come to a general agreement on the impact of something and say whether it is higher than that of another event. This is all that is needed at this stage. To make life easier a score could be assigned to each – Very High = 5, High = 4 etc. These tables are examples and other scoring systems or descriptions could be used, as long as the business management involved agrees. It is a vital step to ensure that this agreement is reached before work starts and it does not matter which method is used.

Probabilities

The second area is the probability or chance of something happening. There is remarkably little real probability data available for most events, even ones which affect populations of people, so for a business a table on which we can find agreement is a better tool than false data. The following table is most commonly used but, as with that for impact, make sure that it is agreed in advance and that everybody uses the same one:

Table 5.1 Probabilities of threats occurring

Probability	Score	Frequency	Qualitative	Likelihood
Very Low	1	Every 3 years	Negligible; 'May occur in exceptional circumstances'	< = 5%
Low	2	Every year	Unlikely; 'Uncommon, but known to occur elsewhere'	6–25%
Medium	3	Every 6 months	Likely; 'Some evidence to suggest this is possible'	26–50%
High	4	Every quarter	Highly likely; 'May occur'	51–80%
Very High	5	Every month	Almost certain; 'Is expected to occur'	> = 81%

Using this table we can either look at a quantitative method (column 3 – frequency of occurrence) or an easier method which is the qualitative method in column 4. Column 5 simply gives some pre-agreed figure for the likelihood which is useful to weight different scenarios (see the practice section). Once more we can score these probabilities and give Very High = 5, High = 4 etc.

This is the final step in risk assessment. Score the impact, score the probability and then multiply the two. So a High Impact event (= 4) with a High Probability (= 4) scores 16 (4 × 4). This risk is to be taken more seriously than a Medium Impact event (= 3) with a Very High Probability (= 5) since its score is 15 (3 × 5). This is rough and ready but it focuses already on those risks you should do something about.

Here is an example of a final risk assessment:

Table 5.2 Probabilities multiplied by impact

Risk scenario	Probability	Impact	Final assessment
Loadbay printer breaks down	1 (Very Low)	4 (High)	$1 \times 4 = 4$
50% staff absent in pandemic	3 (Medium)	5 (Very High)	$3 \times 5 = 15$
Supplier unable to provide rivets on time	2 (Low)	4 (High)	$2 \times 4 = 8$
External net access breaks – no email	2 (Low)	5 (Very High)	$2 \times 5 = 10$

Colour coding the results focuses the attention.

Ignore/reduce or plan

Look at each risk and make a decision on whether it can be ignored (a risk that will be accepted) or reduced by changing either the impact or the probability, or whether a continuity plan needs to be put in place. When risks are prioritised, either by scoring or other methods, it is time to decide what to do about them.

In continuity planning there are three things you can do: ignore them, reduce their impact or prepare a plan for them. This last is usually called a 'business continuity plan'.

Ignoring risks – getting to risk appetite

This is one of the hardest problems to solve. The best you can hope for is some expression such as 'conservative', 'averse' or 'aggressive'. Usually it involves someone making a choice and often this is based on bad information. This leads to the common situation where the appetite for risk is first expressed as zero ('I won't take any risks') until it is pointed out that this might cost a lot. Then the appetite is defined as the amount of risk that can be taken for a set amount of money: 'How much risk will I be taking if I spend X?' The amount spent this way is often calculated based on some 'industry metrics'. If your peer is spending X you should spend X or less. If your industry average is Y you should be close to Y.

This is patently ridiculous. Even if my company is in exactly the same market as a competitor there will always be differences between us in terms of location, people profile, service level etc. and this will lead to differences in market offerings and our customer bases and their expectations. Whilst the approach has some merit in terms of comparability it should stop there, and the assessment of risk appetite should follow after the BIA and the risk analysis and be a separate exercise based on the risks identified.

This way of dealing with risk appetite is based on concrete information. The risk analysis will highlight the risks and impact (and of course only the risks associated with impact other than Low) and then management can make a simple choice of which they accept and which they don't. Unfortunately this step is often overlooked.

Risk appetite is usually expressed in monetary terms but when you ask for the number the answer is often vague. Risk appetite can be expressed in other ways such as 'averse' or 'bold' etc. but this doesn't help much in the crucial process of deciding which risks should be taken and which should not. There is a statutory and common sense requirement to state explicitly the level of risk a company will take. To do this simply list the risks seen, prioritised using one of the methods mentioned, and ask your stakeholders which they accept. The results will be varied but will point to a level which equates to the risk appetite either in monetary terms or others (such as customer satisfaction, regardless of money).

Fixing risks by reducing their impact

During the process of risk analysis and assessment, there will be some risks which can be changed by taking actions. A risk has an impact and a probability. If you can change either the priority of the risk changes, and it may be that it is reduced to the 'ignore' category by taking some mitigating action.

As an example, during risk analysis it is discovered that there is a weakness in the weighbridge printing system. If a printer fails there will be delays in delivery and problems in downstream workflow. Risk assessment with a group of stakeholders decides that this event could occur every six months (due mainly to the dusty and rigorous working conditions) and that the impact would be threefold:

- delays to the first four shipments after the breakdown;
- backup of lorries in the warehouse;
- additional work in informing customers and executing some of the work manually.

The cost of this impact is estimated at £10,000. The risk assessment is High risk due to the impact being quite high and the probability being high (twice per year).

There are choices to be made here. The situation could be left as it is and a continuity plan put in place which, for example, would ensure that a new printer were available in local stock at all times. There would be a cost associated with this and it would establish a procedure to replace the printer quickly if something happened. This would provide continuity and a much smaller delay. This is the business continuity option so to speak.

An alternative choice is to change the probability or the impact and therefore change the risk assessment to a much lower value. For example by installing a dust screen we can reduce the frequency of occurrence to, say, once per year. Another example would be automating part of the work of informing customers. (This could even be done by some form of service level agreement that explicitly states that shipments may arrive without documentation, in which case the document will come two days later; customers may not sign this, of course.) Either or both of these actions combined will reduce the overall rating of the risk from High to, perhaps, Low (since the impact is now lowered to Medium and the probability is Low).

For every risk there is always this form of action to look at. You can change the impact, change the probability – so changing the overall risk rating – or leave these as they are and put in place a continuity procedure.

Good continuity plans always do a combination of both and over time tend to make businesses more efficient because constant risk reduction is in place based on stakeholder feedback.

Planning for a risk occurrence
For those risks where it has been decided that ignoring or reduction won't be acceptable, a plan is made. The idea of a plan is that it is accepted that something is going to happen at some stage for sure, so we pre-plan for this eventuality and document what will happen. This is called a 'scenario' and the entire handling of risks is dealt with this way. Whether it is the loss of a printer or a building the methodology is the same – design a scenario and test it before the risk occurs.

Design scenarios
This step is to express the risk in a scenario form. For example if it is agreed that a threat area is hardware breakdown and the risk is that a printer will break down, then a scenario could be, 'Shipping printer breaks down and is out of service for three hours'. This forces action other than just fixing the printer and is expressed in a form that people understand.

6 SUPPORTING FUNCTIONS FUNCTIONS AND DEPARTMENTS

When we look at the resources a procedure requires there are some which are internal such Human Resources or Finance or IT. These need to be dealt with in a special way since they are not usually revenue centres, so are not 'businesses' we can analyse in the normal Business Impact Analysis way.

A functional department has exactly the same process to follow as the entire business. The difference is that there is no need for a Business Impact Analysis – this is done by the business and assesses business impact. If a support function fails (as one of the business's resources) it is a failure – there is no such idea as to do a risk assessment and decide if the function should work or not work since it is required to work by the business.

For example a line of business requires that some vendor contracts are in place and the support function called Procurement does this. If the contracts are not in place then the business could fail in some circumstances but the business has decided they will be in place. As a support function Procurement does not need to do its own BIA to decide if it should negotiate vendor contracts – this is a requirement from business. Procurement should do its own risk assessment to decide how it is going to provide this service and make it work, and this is usually best done with the support of the overall BCM team (if only to ensure adherence to policy and standards). Each function must do the same to be sure it can supply the services required by business management and must develop scenarios for these risks and procedures to test and execute during outage. Some will be more complex than others; see the suggestions below.

THE SPECIAL CASES OF IT AND FACILITIES

As mentioned above these are both supporting functions, although often they are not treated as such. Indeed many continuity plans simply regard IT continuity as making IT work and able to move to other sites during certain outage cases. The common method of making IT work 'continuously', and thereby avoid continuity problems, is to look towards technical solutions that improve uptime and then to measure this.

For Facilities it is also common only to take protective measures to ensure the availability of the current facilities. Facilities are usually a shared resource for multiple lines of business. There is usually a Facilities manager who will take the actions to protect the facilities but it is incumbent on business management to consider scenarios for business continuity when facilities are not available. Usually there are alternatives and it is short-sighted to take the traditional approach, which aims at protecting the facilities as much as possible against the classic outages such as fire. This is the same as the IT approach which aims at uptime and fails for the same reasons – what do you do when the outages **do** occur? As mentioned previously facilities will be unavailable and IT will break down, so what happens now?

For Facilities ensure that business management considers doing business in some form without the current facilities (such as working from home) and at the same time do what is needed to avoid the loss of the facilities. **Last, if a facility outage occurs (be it access, electricity, heating etc.) it is NOT the fault of the Facilities manager. It is the fault of the business manager who did not design a scenario for such a loss of resource in his business.**

Neither of these areas is a special case in reality. Few businesses or business lines can survive without both IT and Facilities and the protective measures are important. However they should be analysed in exactly the same way as other lines of business with one exception: they generally don't have a revenue number associated with them so they can often be associated with the entire revenue of the business.

However the further process of defining the threats, risks, scenarios and procedures remains the same. IT should take great care to ensure that its approach is not limited to uptime. Many things can prevent IT from working and providing support to business functions. The majority of the serious ones are not technical but organisational or facilities-related, involving people and external support. This is explored in more detail below.

There is sometimes a desire to do a BIA on IT. When you hear this it means that the request is for an analysis of the impact if part of IT breaks down. This is then used to justify the need for that part of IT to have a continuity plan. This is a valid approach as long as the analysis is complete. By this I mean that the entire business impact should be analysed and agreed – which is hard if the initial approach is from the perspectives of IT and business – and that all the outage scenarios should be considered. An IT approach is pretty dangerous for the latter reason.

Consider this case. We have a two-step procedure (very simple!) to fix an outage of a single server. The first step is technical and takes 5 minutes. The second step is a human process and takes 30. Can this be used as a justification for the 5 minute technical step? Probably not. As a result it might be a waste of money.

Consider this case too. IT claims that it needs a remote datacentre to be available for some outages and it is a warm site that needs a bit of starting and a few people. What if there is a transport problem? Clearly someone could have written the procedure to ensure that the transport problem is fixed but it is much easier and more secure to take a business approach and get **all** the stakeholders round a table so that **all** the scenarios and resources are discussed from the beginning. This way we avoid having an imbalance between technology and real business breakdowns and consider all types of outage and their real business impact.

Very often an IT approach is driven by IT because LOB managers will not allocate sufficient budget for IT to be satisfied with its own abilities to recover or provide continuous service. As a result IT does an impact analysis that tries to show which applications are crucial and what needs to be done to maintain their availability. The results are then taken back to business management (which is why applications are the driving point) in an attempt to raise the funding needed. At best this approach is a compromise. The key step should be to ask why LOB managers have not done a BIA so that they can say which business chains are important, which resources are needed (and therefore which applications) and what the impact would be if there were outage events. In other words doing their jobs properly.

So if IT wants to do a continuity plan without the hard evidence provided by a business BIA there is often a problem. The way to tackle this is top-down via the board of management. Remember that, whatever is being spent on IT, it cannot be proven to be the right amount if there has been no BIA and no evidence of the real impact of loss. The same holds true for any support function. As has been mentioned previously, judging the amount to spend on IT by comparing it with similar companies makes no sense whatsoever. It can only be judged within the context of the value of IT to the current business and its need for IT to provide a given service level and a given insurance against loss.

GENERAL ISSUES WITH IT RECOVERY ARCHITECTURES

No book on business continuity would be complete without mention of recovery architectures. What follows is not a treatise on how to build them – which is well known – but a set of arguments as to why they don't solve the business continuity problem and what you need to look out for.

An IT recovery (or disaster recovery) architecture is designed to provide continuous service of the IT function by making it immune to the impact of any risk. If it can be afforded this is usually some combination of IT datacentres, sufficiently far apart not to be affected by the same risks and able to handle the work of any original datacentre with no perceptible loss of service levels. I will leave aside those cases where the DR site is in the same building as the original datacentre, where the network between datacentres is unreliable or slow, or where it is impossible to have sites far enough apart that they are not affected by the same risks. Sadly all of these do happen in practice.

Even assuming this multi-site solution can be afforded, how does it not solve the problem? On the face of it, it should.

Here are three good reasons though there may be others:

Chain of events: IT is only part of any business. How does continuous IT handle a lorry being stuck in snow for example? It doesn't.

Data loss: No matter how much you spend some data will be lost, usually as a result of transmission latency or failure. Since this is guaranteed to happen there needs to be some detailed procedure written to handle it.

Service loss: In an IT system there will be remote devices. For example a bank has remote ATMs interfacing to the unbreakable IT system. How does having an unbreakable IT system help if the ATM fails due to an application bug? It doesn't.

So having a resilient IT system is a good idea if it is needed for the risks identified, but it is not the universal panacea for business continuity. It is quite feasible to build IT architectures with no single points of failure (SPOF) and still fail a BCM audit and have no realistic BCM capability in practice. However the automated management of IT architecture, and the discipline that comes with this, reduce part of the complexity of the chain of events and therefore make the development of business continuity plans easier.

If we take a simple example of the chain of events to provide a business service, there are things which may go wrong, things which will go wrong and things which won't. Here is an example of a banking system where someone wants to withdraw cash from an ATM which is connected to a datacentre with disaster recovery capabilities.

Table 6.1 Failure scenarios for ATM datacentre

Link in the chain	What will go wrong	What may go wrong	What won't go wrong
ATM	ATM application	Everything	ATM power supply?
	ATM operating system		
	ATM hardware		
	ATM physical hardware		
Network connection to the ATM	Telecoms line	Router connection	
Incoming network connection to the datacentre	Telecoms line		Power supply
Internal datacentre network			Internal network
ATM server and its support servers	Hardware	Swapover processes to a remote site	
	Operating system software	People	
	Application used		

This is not complete but for any chain of events it can help to develop such a map. This is because for each entry there needs to be a defined plan to handle the breakdown – especially the column, 'What will go wrong'.

IT CONSIDERATIONS

This section covers some of the considerations per support function.

- Ensure that home working is in place technically for required staff including telecoms bandwidth and the required equipment (PCs, modems, credentials etc.). IT defines this according to the LOB stated needs in terms of staff numbers but the LOB pays for it and Finance approves it.

- Ensure that the continuity of IT is assured. This means networking and applications together with the required level of support.

- Scenarios which IT should develop for itself include:

    (a) hardware component failure;

    (b) software component failure;

    (c) application failure;

    (d) vendor support loss;

    (e) reduced availability of staff for a number of days;

    (f) malicious infrastructure attack;

    (g) loss of access to part of the datacentre;

    (h) loss of internet access;

    (i) loss of local connectivity requiring failover to another site;

    (j) loss of staff worldwide due to disease;

    (k) loss of a complete datacentre.

- To be clear about the above scenarios list consider application failure as an example. Obviously an application is a specific resource for a specific line of business so it can be argued that, unless that business requests that application failure be planned for, nothing should be done. Strictly speaking this is true but common sense says that a bare minimum framework for all of these scenarios needs to be in place anyway because they will always be required. For example you would always have a procedure to change hardware after failure, regardless of what business asked for. Consider these the baselines. It is a bit like running a taxi service: you would always keep the oil level in your car correct and have spare wheels even if your client didn't ask for it.

PROCUREMENT CONSIDERATIONS

- Ensure vendors have a business continuity plan in place and arrange an audit as needed.

- Ensure that vendor contracts include business continuity explicitly. This means that the contract with each vendor mentions the existence of a continuity capability and the right to either see or audit it. Procurement should also highlight those vendors which do not conform to this so that management can decide whether to change vendors or provide arrangements with alternative vendors. If a vendor cannot or will not guarantee the ability to keep going during an outage then an alternative is to increase stock of the vendor product with the agreement of management. This will not work for services so alternative vendors is the only choice. The outage scenarios that the vendor should cover should be provided by the BCM team rather than the vendor. Typically the types of scenarios vendors should be able to respond to will be these:

  (a) providing support (repair, response etc.) within a certain time;

  (b) providing a product within a certain time.

- Ensure that the ability to purchase is covered by emergencies. This means that some provision or process must be in place to ensure emergency purchase. Whilst this needs agreement from Accounting and Finance the process should be driven by Procurement management. When an outage occurs there is not always going to be time to follow a process to gain sign-off for purchase.

- Scenarios which Procurement should develop for itself include:

  (a) loss of 50% of staff;

  (b) loss of office facilities (where do their staff work?);

  (c) loss of network access and phones.

HUMAN RESOURCE CONSIDERATIONS

- Ensure that internal staff are trained and able to cover alternative jobs in the event of an outage, and that there is a system in place whereby personnel can be found from internal resources and assigned to alternative tasks. A manager writing a scenario for loss of staff will need to rely upon HR to get the staff needed.

- Ensure that alternative sources of staff are available externally. Whilst the contractual side is dealt with by Procurement, HR has to determine the needs from management and define who the external suppliers of staff will be. The external staff will usually be contractors or agency staff although arrangements could be made for service provision from agencies. For example instead of taking staff on-site for support desk work, the staff could be at an outsourcing site.

57

- Scenarios which HR should develop for itself include:

  (a) loss of 50% of own staff;

  (b) loss of 50% of all staff due to illness;

  (c) pandemic plan where 50% of staff are ill with contagious disease;

  (d) loss of office facilities;

  (e) loss of network access and phones;

  (f) loss of primary or secondary staff suppliers.

Pandemic and loss of staff planning

Probably the key area where HR contributes is in scenarios where staff numbers are reduced. There are many events that can lead to the loss of staff on a short- or medium-term basis and HR provides the support both to management and staff when this happens.

Typical events leading to the loss of staff are personal illness, direct industrial action, indirect industrial action such as transport strikes and collective illnesses such as pandemics.Each is a threat and each has an associated probability and resultant business risk. Each should have typical scenarios defined and procedures written in advance by business management. It is not the job of HR to write these plans. HR should support the plans as defined above (i.e. by providing the means by which management can get the staff they need within local labour regulations).

Pandemic is not really any different. A pandemic is a loss of staff situation with a few differences. The major ones are these:

- It affects all departments of a business as well as all the business's suppliers and customers.

- It affects travel. People won't travel out of fear or can't travel due to health warnings from a government.

- It requires longer-term planning because the outage may last months rather than days.

- It is likely to affect a high percentage of staff.

- It requires a lot of communication with staff as well as customers.

- It requires some hygiene actions in coordination with local medical agencies. This affects visitors to buildings, visitors from other countries (perhaps due to quarantine) and staff movement to and from work.

- It requires planning to allow staff to work remotely and this has effects on equipment and technology (such as remote access).

- It will most likely require reporting internally and externally.

A key element in pandemic planning is the requirement to plan for a change in how business is done. Usually business continuity tries to keep the business running in some form, either by restoring services or providing alternatives. In a pandemic consideration has to be given to stopping parts of the business on a semi-permanent basis and this can have far-reaching consequences. As an example, if delivery must be stopped because lorry drivers are ill, what happens to production? If production is semi-automated, what happens to the goods produced and where are they stocked?

However pandemic planning is no different from planning for any other scenario – it requires looking at the scenario and designing procedures to execute. It may only appear to be more dramatic because of the potentially high numbers of staff absent and the fear that it can engender. So far the pandemic threats have been relatively benign and there could clearly be more virulent and dangerous pandemics to come. However the way they are dealt with from a continuity point of view does not change.

FACILITIES CONSIDERATIONS

- Ensure that the facilities function as planned and agreed. This means that all of the normal requirements for heat, light, safety and power are in place with the ability to withstand normal scenarios. Hence alternative power supply generators would normally be available together with adequate fuel supplies. Alternative heating and light should be available.

- Ensure that internal IT plans and procedures for alternative facilities are in place. This is slightly different from an office staffing plan since some of the sub-functions of IT can be removed to alternative sites without staff, or outsourced. Whatever plan IT have for this the facilities side is not their responsibility.

- Ensure that each LOB gives the staffing levels required during outage and any special requirements for these staff in terms of space and location.

- Ensure that alternative facilities are available for office staff and, in conjunction with IT, for datacentre equipment and people. Whilst the need is driven by IT the actual provisioning, agreement and installation is driven by the Facilities function, with contracts agreed with Procurement and signed by Finance.

- Define the procedures whereby loss of any Facilities function is handled. This will usually involve moving some staff to another location and some to home working (if provided), and ensuring the safety and security of the facilities and staff throughout. Transport is also part of this responsibility.

- Scenarios which Facilities should develop for itself include:

  (a) loss of 50% staff;

  (b) loss of network and phone access;

  (c) loss of main offices;

(d) loss of datacentre facilities;

(e) staff evacuation procedures;

(f) fire drills;

(g) staff hygiene and facilities hygiene.

FINANCE CONSIDERATIONS

- Ensure that the administrative processes are in place for emergency purchase during outage with the correct reconciliation later. The requirement, levels and emergency sign-off ability are driven in conjunction with Procurement and LOB management.

- Scenarios which Finance should develop for itself include:

(a) loss of 50% staff;

(b) loss of network and phone access.

7   SCENARIOS

A scenario is a description of a type of event which is expressed in simple, normal language such as, 'Access to the building is denied to all staff'. In this scenario it doesn't really matter why the access is denied and there could be multiple reasons, but it still comes down to the same thing.

A scenario is something that ordinary people can understand, which reflects what can happen in real life, which can be tested simply and which is a materialisation of a real risk.

The common approach to this phase is to express such things as, 'The probability of such an event happening is X% or High, Medium, Low'. This approach suffers from many flaws – the primary ones are that it invites discussion of the percentage or rating used and that it does not relate to real life. If we look at the above scenario (denial of access), it is far easier to understand that access is denied than that the chances of access being denied are 'Medium'!

For each risk there should be at least one scenario developed and simply expressed. Developing scenarios should be done with stakeholders and it is often more fruitful to use scenarios as a means of looking at risks, since stakeholders know what may go wrong but sometimes have difficulty expressing these as risks in the formal sense. Another good reason for this approach is that the people involved in the risk assessments may not be the people on the ground. If you need to know the risks involved in shipping operations, asking the people in the warehouse sometimes gives results that the management may have overlooked, and which are often invisible because the people in the warehouse use some unofficial workaround. There is more on this in the risk section.

Here are some examples of scenarios which can happen to any business:

- Invoices can't be printed.
- Deliveries leave the depot late.
- Half the office PCs break down.
- 40% of staff don't come into the office for three days.

In all cases the events causing these scenarios are irrelevant – the net result is usually the same.

Scenarios should be developed by the BCM leader with the active participation of the people running the various parts of a business. This is the only way to ensure that there is agreement and acceptance, and that the scenarios accurately reflect all the types of outages that can occur in all areas of a business. Having 100% reliability in IT and Accounting and a 100% reliable office building will not help if people are late for work or there is a tanker driver strike so there is no diesel for the delivery lorries.

The key to getting scenarios is stakeholder involvement. Good scenarios reflect real life events that have happened (or could), and which represent something that can be played out or tested. A procedure is developed for a scenario and this forms the basis of a test.

SCENARIOS AND CAPABILITY

A scenario provides another benefit. If it represents a real type of event running it in a test environment will give a good indication of the company's real capability in terms of recovery time. Running the associated procedure live will give an even better idea.

For a particular business line (be it product, service or service chain – defined earlier) there will be multiple risks and scenarios, and therefore multiple procedures. Each procedure will give a different recovery time capability (RTC) so it remains to determine the 'composite' RTC. This is done quite simply. Each procedure will have a different recovery time and each procedure represents a risk with a different chance of happening.

For example the business line we are looking at is called Client Spares. This line has its own P&L, so it is accounted for separately for multiple reasons. It has its own management and, as a business line, it covers the production of spares and their stocking, ordering and shipment to customers, together with the associated invoicing (which is a shared resource with other lines).

Anything in this business line which breaks can affect the recovery time capability of the line. A risk analysis has raised a number of issues represented by the scenarios below and each scenario has a procedure which has been tested and which gives the RTC below.

Table 7.1 Examples of risk scenarios

1	2	3	4
Risk scenario	Recovery time capability	Risk probability	Weighted result
Printer in shipping fails	2 hours	40% or 0.4	0.8 hours
Production line fails so X spares cannot be made	3 hours	10% or 0.1	0.3 hours
Smoke damage in the shipping area	1 hour	10% or 0.1	0.1 hours
		0.6	1.2 hours

Now we have applied a weighting to each scenario based upon the chances of its happening. We can now calculate the recovery time capability of this line of business as a weighted average using this formula:

$$(RTC1 * l1 + RTC2 * l2 + \ldots + RTCn * ln) / (l1 + l2 + \ldots + ln)$$

(Where **RTCn** is the recovery time capability measured for scenario **n** and **ln** is the probability of scenario **n** happening.)

For each scenario multiply the capability by the probability: this gives column 4 – 1.2 hours; take the sum of all the probabilities: sum of column 3 = 0.6; then divide the first by the second: 1.2/0.6 = 2 hours.

The same formula is used if you have 20 scenarios with 20 different recovery time capabilities. The hard part is agreeing the probability and hence the weighting. This is not an exact exercise for reasons previously cited – there is little or no objective probability data for the vast majority of events.

Use this weighted average as a reasonably good guide to capability. If the number is too high (since its being low is unlikely to cause problems) there can be multiple reasons. These include the probabilities being too pessimistic, the weighting system which translates from High/Medium/Low to a probability being askew, and the recovery times for the scenarios being wrong (for example because the BCM procedures need review). However the weighted average will give a pretty good idea and should be used as a guide only.

8 PROCEDURES – THE LAST THING TO DO IS THINK

A procedure is defined as a set of steps to undertake when something goes wrong. The word '**procedure**' is used to differentiate from the word '**process**', which is used in many areas in many ways.

A procedure should be written so that someone unfamiliar with the situation can execute it and get the desired result. It should not require the input of an expert in the particular domain in order to work.

A procedure is written for a particular scenario. There should be one for each scenario and obviously there should be a scenario for every risk. In this way there are instructions for every risk that has been identified. These will evolve over time and, as new risk assessments are done, new risks will emerge and old ones may be excluded. New scenarios will be developed and new procedures developed for each.

Most important, procedures can be tested – this can be done by simulation or live tests – but this is discussed in more detail in the next section.

Here is a template that can be used to define a procedure:

Table 8.1 Procedure table

Process step	Who does it	Time taken	Resource needed	Comments

The columns are completed as follows:

Process step: A single, definable and measurable action. As an example, 'Send request to shipping department contact X'. A bad example would be, 'Inform shipping'. In this one it is not clear who is to be informed, which leads to ambiguity.

Who: This should be the name of the person or the role. There should be an annex document with all of the current contacts.

Time taken: How long will this step take. This can be a maximum or minimum number. By definition the time sequence of this procedure is top-down. The third step happens after the second – it cannot happen before – and must be completed before step four. This data will also give an **estimate** of how long outages will take to resolve, by adding up the values in this column.

Resource needed: The word 'resource' is used in the widest sense. If the resource needed is a document then the name and location of the document should be here. If the resource is a person then that person's name and contact details should be here. If the resource is IT equipment then the exact definition should be here. As mentioned before a person unfamiliar with this procedure should be able to execute it.

Here is a completed example for a scenario where a steel company is shipping bulk steel which needs to pass a weighbridge, and the actual shipped weight is printed and attached to the shipment. The customer's business depends on this weight since they onward ship themselves, so it is deemed to be very important.

Table 8.2 Example procedure

Scenario: Shipping documentation server fails so some shipments will not have weight details

#	Process step	Who	Time taken	Resource needed	Comments
1	Contact customers to inform them of the outage and that weights will be given by mail initially	Current shift manager from the shift rota located in the service area	20 minutes average for all the current customers	Current customer list located either on the current BCM DVD or sales server host INV003/SALES/CLIENTS	Contact will be done by phone first and with confirmation by email second

Table 8.2 *(Continued)*

Scenario: Shipping documentation server fails so some shipments will not have weight details

#	Process step	Who	Time taken	Resource needed	Comments
2	Remove server from network	Operations shift manager	10 minutes	Operations shift team	This step and the following steps can start in parallel with the first step
3	For each shipment record the actual weight	Weighbridge foreman	3 minutes per shipment	Weight logbook updated on INV003/SALES/ LOGBOOK Record details	
4	Inform customers of weights from the logbook	Sales rep for each customer	n/a	Use logbook located on server INV003/Sales/ LOGBOOK and updated in real time. Use email addresses from server in step 1	
5	Rebuild server	Operations shift manager	3 hours	Rebuild instructions located on DVD and located on server SUPPORT/ REBUILD	This step may take less time than planned

This procedure is far from complete but so far it contains all the details needed for an uninitiated person to be able to run it.

Of course for this to be usable there needs to be an additional document referring to contacts and substitutes like this:

Table 8.3 Example of procedure contacts list

Role	Contact	Email	Phones	Substitutes
Weighbridge foreman	John Smith	js@business.com	01556-5589 Mob: 022-592-481	Michael James
	Michael James	mj@business.com	01487-2338 Mob: 022-592-439	None
Operations shift manager	Refer to rota located at OPS/ROTA/SHIFT Operations manager responsible for all shifts is David Jones	dj@business.com	01376-3371 Mob: 022-328-338	None

From a quality point of view a procedure should conform to these guidelines:

- Based on the procedure document and the documents referenced from the procedure, is it clear for each step of the procedure who **exactly** will do what, when, where and how?

- Is there an unambiguously defined **individual** for each step who is responsible for that step? (Team responsibility is not sufficient and leads to confusion.)

- Are the steps described in a way that even a third-level backup person can execute it? (Bearing in mind that that person is not necessarily involved in the particular service.)

- Are backup (substitute) persons defined for each role?

- Are contact details included for substitutes?

- If there are more detailed (technical) activities behind the procedure steps, are they clearly referenced from the procedure? (In most cases it is not sufficient just to refer to a document – page numbers or section numbers should be used to precisely identify the particular step.)

- Are the steps and the detailed activities described in a way that is easy to read and executable in any situation?

- Are all roles referenced from the procedure steps defined in an information tab?

- Are all defined roles, contacts, etc. really used (i.e. referred to) in the procedure steps?
- If a step is passed over to another person or function:
  - (a) Is there a sub-step to make sure that the step **can be** done? (To ensure that the required resources are available and it's acknowledged that the sub-step is being taken over.)
  - (b) Is there a clear time frame defined for the step being passed over?
  - (c) Is there a sub-step to make sure that the step **has been** done?
  - (d) Is the condition for resuming the procedure defined?
- No steps should be dead ends.
- No assumptions should be made unless they are documented as assumptions or conditions.

IT PROCEDURES

If we look at step 5 in the above procedure there is a process step called 'Rebuild Server'. This could be one of many steps which IT may need to execute. For each of these IT process steps there should be a documented IT procedure (sometimes called a 'Run Book' or something similar).

Such an IT procedure should be documented like any other to a level of detail enabling any IT operator to execute it. These procedures should be stored in just the same way as BCM procedures (offline and online copies kept up-to-date by IT Operations).

This level of discipline is very easy to overlook and it is often assumed that IT Operations know how to do things such as rebuilding a server. For example if the process step was, 'Rebuild server and restart application', things would be more complex. When the application restarts, where does it restart from? Which data does it use and which data is lost? These matters are outside the domain of competence of IT Operations and require a business decision. Only by ensuring rigorous levels of documentation can such a situation be clarified.

The IT procedures domain is not a special case as such. It is highlighted because IT plays such an important role in most companies and is usually staffed by experts, so the level of documentation discipline sometimes tends to be lax.

9 TESTING AND STAYING FRIENDS

Running tests is the one sure way to annoy people at all levels and lose any remaining support you may have for your BCM programme. Testing takes time and consumes resources but it is important to remember that you will be testing **their** procedures, not yours. Testing is running a procedure to see if it gives the expected result. It should also look for a relationship between the scenario and the written procedure.

Testing disrupts business even if it is desk testing – live testing will always be cited as a requirement by management but doing it is another matter. It should happen as procedures are developed and then, in some form, on a regular basis to satisfy auditors. This can be every year – some auditors might accept every two years – and is usually referred to as, 'Exercising the plan'. What is actually tested and how (desk or live) is usually the subject of negotiation between management, the BCM project manager and the auditors, and there is no hard and fast rule defining what to do.

There are three levels of test:

IN-DEPTH ANALYSIS

The stakeholders who write continuity procedures are the main target here. Never assume that, just because they know the procedures they would implement to recover from an outage, they will also write procedures which make sense, are logical in sequence and work in practice. Someone from the BCM team needs to review and analyse the procedures and have a quality checklist as shown previously. Do this formally and give written feedback so that procedures can be updated and reviewed again until agreement is reached.

During analysis it can be that the procedure highlights things not discovered in the BIA. Look for these types of thing:

- The procedure works but is recovered in an unrealistic timeframe (too long or short).

- The procedure includes decisions but the party who could make the decision does not know he is involved even though, on paper, the procedure works. As an example, when a network failure occurs, a decision needs to be made by security people, but they either cannot or will not make such a decision.

- The procedure is recovering from a scenario when, in fact, the scenario requires no recovery but instead an alternative method of providing continuity. Sometimes there will be a conflict between the BIA results and the scenarios.

DESK TESTING

A desk test is the least intrusive form of actual testing. It involves walking through a procedure with the people who would be involved. Clearly there are a number of common sense steps to deal with around logistics. Everyone mentioned in a BCM procedure should be invited but they will not all be able to attend and may not physically be able to send a deputy. This is acceptable as long as they are reachable by another communications method, as would be the case in practice. Plan for a procedure desk test to take a couple of hours.

Here is the process:

- The person who wrote the procedure should go through it step by step.
- Assign someone to take notes.
- Assign someone (usually a BCM team member) to be the 'auditor' who will require proof that each step works.
- For each step there will be an action and someone to execute it.
- For each action the team should agree how long it would take in practice (this can often be a range as opposed to a single figure).
- If people are to be contacted by phone, call them and see what happens in reality. (The same applies to mail contacts.)
- If people cannot be contacted try their deputies. If this does not work it is cause for failure.
- When all the steps have been executed any single-step failure means the entire procedure fails, so corrective action needs to be taken.

Here is an example with results:

Table 9.1 Example of desk test results

#	Process step	Who	Estimated time for this step	Resource/ explanation	Comments	Pass/fail
1	Contact remote site manager		10 minutes	Contact using list SITE-LIST.DOC	List is available with names and contacts	Pass

Table 9.1 *(Continued)*

#	Process step	Who	Estimated time for this step	Resource/ explanation	Comments	Pass/fail
2	Staff move to alternate site		90 minutes	Take taxis to the remote site	Called the taxi company and there were none available so either this would take longer in practice or a contract should be signed for priority service	Fail (in practice)
3	Install PCs on the network to provide support		30 minutes	Staff take their own portable PCs to the remote site and install them personally	The name of the local network administrator is missing from the contacts sheet in case there are connectivity issues so this could cause a problem	Fail
	TOTAL		130 minutes			

From this desk test it can be seen that there are a number of small comments which need correction. Depending upon their severity it would not be needed in this case to rerun such a test. The total column gives a rough idea of how long this would take in practice but it might need validation by a live test. In a lot of cases the combined experience of the people running these tests would be sufficient for the numbers to be fair, so don't go looking for work.

LIVE TESTING

Do this partially with half the target team in case anything goes wrong, in which case the entire service is wrecked. Full-scale live tests, unannounced, are not worth the effort for the return you get even if you get agreement (which is unlikely).

Live testing will be testing a procedure for a scenario. Let's take as an example the move to an alternate site for a support service when their original site has been made unusable.

Split the team running the service in two so that half will continue to provide normal service, albeit with some reduction in service levels possible. For the other half of the team live testing should execute the BCM procedure, just the same as with a desk test except that the actions take place. As an example three steps from this procedure which shows the difference between a desk test and a live test. The live test actually executes the action when possible. Time the actual step duration and note it.

Table 9.2 Differences between desk test and live test actions

Step	Desk test actions	Time taken 'desk'	'Live' test actions	Time taken 'live'
Contact remote site manager	Estimate as a team how long a call would take		Call him. If no answer call the deputy. If no answer the step and procedure fail. Time how long it takes	
Staff move to alternate site	Estimate the time this will take and ensure that the site is available when requested		Staff go to the site and knock on the door. Time how long this takes	
Install PCs on the network to provide support	Estimate as a team how long this takes		Staff take their own PCs to the remote site and install them on the network and time how long it takes	
TOTAL				(Total)

This type of live test is the least disruptive, since live work is going on in parallel, and it also provides more accurate figures of the time it will take to execute each step. The total time on the right will provide an upper bound to the time it would take in practice, so it serves to check if the procedure is acceptable in practice. If not then the steps need to be changed, or the procedure needs redesigning, or the individual time required for steps must be improved. One outcome of live testing, which may not come from desk testing or in-depth review, is that the whole procedure can identify an alternative way of doing things. It is a common mistake to assume that a procedure must reinstate a situation exactly as it was before rather than providing another way of doing things.

10 AUDIT

An audit is about past performance and current intentions. Nothing will ever be 100% complete so go into an audit with this in mind and present what has been done, what is being done and what is going to be done. This is reality. This section looks at some simple preparation for external audit. In this context 'external' means external to the continuity function – the auditors could be internal or external.

An audit will review two major areas. The first is the general project management of the BCM project and normal, professional project management will cover this. The second is capability. It is quite possible that a project is well-run and even finished but there is no capability in place in reality. There are multiple reasons for arriving at this situation and one of the major ones is focusing on the content of the project plan too much. When doing project planning it is easy to document and plan the steps towards the objective but very easy to forget the details and the soft details. Here is an example:

Major step (easy to remember to do):

Design recovery procedures for scenarios.

First level of detail:

- Assist stakeholders to design procedures.
- Check procedures against a quality checklist.
- Provide documented feedback.
- Ensure stakeholders update procedures.
- Run desk tests.

Soft detail that is easy to forget:

- Ensure all stakeholders understand and accept the procedures.
- Integrate procedures into incident management processes.
- Ensure stakeholders are trained on the procedures.
- Negotiate and agree procedure update processes.

Whilst these soft details are obvious enough they are not usually that obvious in the beginning, especially when they seem to be out of the scope of the original project. The term 'soft' is used in this context to cover all of those details which are to do with influencing people to use the results of the project. This is because there are essentially no companies where things are done by dictatorship: even the most draconian management styles tend to assume that people will do as they are told and, of course, they never do. The project manager's job is to ensure that the results (interim and final) are used and well integrated into normal operations. This part is easy to overlook.

So audit will be looking for clear signs of capability in terms of how the organisation will react to incidents where business continuity is at stake. This will include how major risks identified in the BIA have been reviewed and mitigated.

Auditors will assume there is a BCM policy and strategy and will need to see evidence of both. The policy is usually easy but the strategy will draw more questions. The strategy will already start to call management judgment into question, since it will define what will be done in certain circumstances. Auditors have the right and duty to comment upon this but you can't fail an audit if they disagree – all that you can get is an audit comment.

Auditors will usually start with the BIA. There needs to be one but, as in strategy, the management prerogative is to decide what to do about risk. If a BIA decides to do nothing about a risk or type of risk, auditors can comment and compare this decision with other industries or market positions but cannot disagree. Bear this in mind when preparing audit documents.

TEST LOGS

Auditors will require evidence of testing at the very least. During the process of designing scenarios and procedures there will be multiple passes or reviews and then desk tests and possibly live tests. The dates and results of each need to be documented somewhere as both an audit chain of evidence and a repository that should be updated in the future as new scenarios are designed and new procedures implemented and tested. Everyone involved should know where this repository is and how to update it. This repository is then a piece of audit evidence that will show when procedures were tested. It does not matter from an audit point of view if they failed, as long as there is a set of notes stating what corrective actions must take place as a result and when.

STAKEHOLDER MANAGEMENT

Do not assume stakeholders know or care about audit. They have a day job so it is unlikely to be their top priority. However stakeholders will be interviewed and you should make sure that they say the right thing individually and as a group.

Remember that if a person does not know the answer to a question this is likely to be interpreted negatively. For example if an auditor asks when BCM procedures are updated and the stakeholder is unsure this will be interpreted as, '**Stakeholders do not update procedures**', rather than being translated as a communications problem. It is not that stakeholders will deliberately tell lies, but they need to be prepared.

So there are two things that need to be done to prepare all the stakeholders prior to an audit. An audit preparation guide should be written and distributed six months in advance and a much shorter FAQ prepared a month beforehand.

Audit preparation guide

This document should cover the BCM programme briefly and define the responsibilities of individuals in detail. When written it should be distributed to all stakeholders and then the major stakeholders should be interviewed to be sure they understand their responsibilities. After all it is their audit, not yours alone.

FAQ

Just prior to an audit prepare a simple FAQ. There will have been enough feedback to understand the types of question people are uncertain about. In the same document remind people where things are located (such as test logs). Remind people of their responsibilities as well and tell them the most important thing – if they don't know a answers for sure say so and refer the auditors to their bosses.

AUDITING YOURSELF

Before and auditor comes in to review, review yourself to see if the plans and management are working as expected. Doing such an audit helps everyone – the stakeholders, you and the internal and external auditors. Doing a self-review is a lightweight exercise which can be done over an extended period but which can act as an ongoing checklist. A self-review does not need to be formalised or done in a fixed time period either.

If the BCM team has a number of staff then this exercise can be distributed amongst team members. It is actually done better via informal methods since formality allows people time to prepare and present the answers they know that an audit will look for. The informal method using 'walkabout management' is more effective and honest and less intrusive, and will give an immediate view of the current status. If the BCM team has few or no staff this exercise will simply take longer.

Here is a checklist of things you need to look at with some hints on how to do each:

(i) Review the current BCM policy and its implementation in practice. Assess the content and validity of the current policy. Assess the communication of the policy.

- The policy should apply to everyone. If ever there are exceptions it is a badly designed and implemented policy. Assume the policy is well-designed andask a random selection of staff what they think of it. If they have never heard of it you know there is a problem somewhere. Like most of this exercise it can be done over coffee or lunch, or just by stopping by desks.

(ii) Assess actual implementation of BCM Strategy within the organisation.

- Fewer people will be affected by the strategy since only a few will be charged with implementing it. Strategy statements usually – or should – define how things are implemented and how customers are affected. Typical questions here sound innocent enough: 'Do our customers appreciate the continuity statements in our service level agreements?'; 'Do you think it is a good idea to have continuity done this way for your product line?'

- These questions depend entirely upon the strategy statement which we will assume exists. As previously mentioned some strategies may cover how things are implemented in some detail and some may cover the way customers are affected. Read the strategy statement if you didn't write it and base the questions on this.

(iii) Assess internal communication, training and awareness methods, content, scope and implementation.

- Everyone should know about what the company is doing in BCM and most should have followed, or be about to follow, some training or awareness. Simply ask people what they thought of the training or if they think some awareness campaigning could be done better. A blank stare is bad news!

(iv) Assess the current methods and results of the Business Impact Analysis.

- A BIA is run by business managers. Ask them if they feel their business is taking unnecessary risks or if they feel comfortable with the current situation. This is an indirect test of whether they think the BIA serves any purpose and whether it has actually been done.

(v) Review the Business impact Analysis and how/whether current RTOs and RPOs align with expectations.

- Include the same people as above but include some staff who deal face-to-face with customers or who sell or design products. Ask support people too, to see how this is implemented in practice. A recovery objective ultimately needs to satisfy customers. Typical questions: 'How long does it take to fix a problem when it happens?'; 'Do your competitors do it any more quickly?'

(vi) Review the current threats and risks to determine if they provide coverage as seen by best practice.

- The people most able to give a decent view on this are in operational roles. For example a lorry drive will tell you more about risks to delivery than anyone else. Simply ask Operations people what is the biggest risk they face and check later against the risk analysis and the scenarios to see if it is covered.

(vii) Review pandemic preparedness plans and comment on their suitability.

- You are the best judge of this since you should know exactly what to do and where to find the information you need. HR should have helped to write the plan so you could ask, for example, if there have been any problems getting medical supplies, or to see the stock out of interest. You don't need to go as far as feigning illness to test this. There ought to be an easily accessible internal website for employees where you can find out what to do if you fall ill.

(viii) Review/audit a sample of risk scenarios.

- Ask to see a couple and see if they make sense. The less you know about these the better you will be able to judge them because they should be written in plain language.

(ix) Audit scope, content, structure, clarity and implementation of a sample of continuity procedures.

- Ask to see one or two and then call some of the people who should be mentioned as resources and whose phone numbers should be in the procedure and ask them what they do when they get a call.

(x) Review any existing plans for complex scenarios such as disasters.

- This is a more complex area and, in spite of best efforts to make disaster plans just as simple and structured as any other risk scenario, you will probably find that there are plans already in existence. It is fairly unlikely that an entire BCM capability has been developed recently, so somewhere there may be plans for what are called 'disasters'. The majority of these will be technical plans to swap IT processing to another site and recover later. It is less likely that full-scale plans for the loss of buildings or people will exist but you never know your luck!

- Ask what happened the last time the plan was used. The answer will be very telling. There is no need to undertake a formal review of such a plan in this exercise: this can and should be done when the plans are updated and reviewed in the yearly cycle. If there is a plan (or plans) it is natural that they would not work properly but they certainly should deal with the scenario they are meant to cover. A loss of building plan has to consider the people, injuries, movement of work, security of the site and information, public and internal communications, recovery and so on. Such a plan should be built using the same process as any other risk scenario procedure.

(xi) Audit test review methodology, content and results.

- Ask to see the test log. It should exist and if it does this is sufficient. It is unlikely to be up-to-date because it is a continuous exercise, so existence is the main thing.

(xii) Audit BCM lifecycle implementation.

- Ask the stakeholders who should be involved (product and service managers and business managers) when their next continuity plan update is scheduled.

11 IMPLEMENTATION AND GOVERNANCE

A GOVERNANCE FRAMEWORK

Business continuity metrics are always shared. Depending upon the organisation the people with the metrics and the objectives will change but no single person has the objective of 'business continuity'. There may be some people in the organisation with job titles relating to continuity, such as a business continuity manager, but this does not preclude this framework. Such a person will never have the time, scope or authority to execute the tasks which belong to business managers for example (such as developing scenarios and procedures).

Here is a matrix of examples of roles and objectives and how to measure them and when:

Table 11.1 Responsibilities of mangers for business continuity

Responsible role	Objective	Measure	Frequency of measurement
Product manager	Execute a Business Impact Analysis for the product line	100% compliance	Yearly
Facilities manager	Test alternative facilities plans	Documented evidence of tests	Yearly
Department managers	Maintain critical staff lists for minimum operations	Documented	Quarterly
All staff	Follow computer based training on BCM	100% compliance	Yearly
Delivery drivers	Review alternative working schedules	100% compliance	As required

Such a list should cover every function within a company and reflect the organisation chart. If there is a box on the organisation chart which does not have a corresponding BCM objective there is probably something wrong.

By doing this exercise we can give an executable task to each person, which can be clearly completed and which they know in advance will be checked. Hence this table serves as a communications tool as well – people can see what they should do, what others will do and when they will all be checked by some internal audit group.

The job descriptions of each role should be changed to reflect these needs, otherwise the governance framework will not work in practice. Obviously doing this requires synchronisation with the Human Resources function.

JOB DESCRIPTIONS

Here is an example of a job description. Every role in the governance framework needs to have an annex or addition to its job description which clearly cites the tasks needed to support continuity management. This does not have to be long and complicated.

Table 11.2 Breakdown of product manager's role in business continuity

	Key activities	**Overall goals/typical measures**
Product manager	Manage the updating of business continuity plans on a yearly basis	Business Impact Analysis is executed yearly or when major new threats appear
		Risk scenarios are developed and agreed for retained risks
		BCM procedures are developed for scenarios
		BCM procedures are tested (desk and live) yearly
		BCM plans are updated
		Mitigation plans are developed when capabilities do not meet minimum market or customer requirements
		Process of BCM audit is managed for internal and external audit

Table 11.2 *(Continued)*

Key activities	Overall goals/typical measures
BCM capabilities communicated	BCM capabilities are communicated to management
	BCM capabilities are communicated to customer representatives
	Customer SLAs are updated
Align with processes and governance	All BCM services are supplied in line with BCM standards

INCIDENT AND ESCALATION MANAGEMENT

This section is included here since it is part of the integration into normal business operations and is often overlooked. Businesses all have some form of process to handle incidents and escalation and the key task here is to integrate with the existing processes rather than designing from scratch.

Incident management is usually fairly well-designed and some kind of service desk and ticketing system can be expected. The following issues need to be addressed and suggested answers are in line:

• Where should BCM be included in incident resolution?

  BCM should not be a normal part of incident resolution. BCM often includes the need for alternatives to be considered and should address business continuity from end to end, whereas incidents in the majority of cases are resolvable fairly simply. Incidents are almost always resolved by fixing problems in a specified time ('fixing' in the sense of not looking at alternatives) so it seems rather excessive to encumber a smooth-running incident management system with the need to have predefined BCM procedures for everything.

• Who should invoke BCM?

  In every company someone is responsible for business lines. This same person is responsible for the BIA for that line and by definition should be responsible for putting in place all components of the business line, including support and therefore incidents. In most companies this will be a product manager of some description. If it is not then the business line manager should be allocated. Clearly this is dependent upon the organisational structure. During incident resolution a support team will eventually be called upon to resolve an incident and should have pre-written BCM procedures at their disposal, as one of the tools to resolve incidents. If an incident is resolved this way then the procedure itself will (or should) include any extraordinary customer facing activities as a result. It is a good idea to fine-tune the incident management process so that the LOB manager can be called upon during the decision process to determine if the BCM procedure should be invoked or not.

- What triggers should invoke BCM procedures?

If an incident cannot be resolved in a contracted time there should either be a continuity procedure to provide an alternative or a communications procedure to the customer or customer agent stating that it will not be resolved. There is no reason to make it more complex than this.

- What happens if there are no procedures written?

Put this down to Lessons Learned and use the incident as experience to write them. There is a good chance that some scenario BCM procedure similar to the one causing the incident will already have been written.

- What should the customer interface be?

Continuity ought to be hidden from the customer and simply be part of the escalation chain. If it is exposed to a customer then the service desk in the future will get nothing but calls from customers demanding extraordinary actions such as a BCM procedure when it is not required. In any event it is not the customer's judgment as to what action should be taken when an incident occurs. (Harsh but true.)

- If an incident is not resolved how is this handled?

This is where Communications comes in. If it can't be resolved and there are no alternatives then the first thing to do is tell the customer(s). Failure to do this quickly or even when it is fairly sure that the incident can't be resolved is one of the major causes of customer dissatisfaction in all industries. Put some procedure in place to inform customers immediately. Part of this should be a single point of contact in the customer business and a single one in your business. Both should be trained to handle these situations, where emotions tend to run high.

- How is escalation triggered?

This is an incident management judgment but the usual trigger is when the service level the customer expects is not going to be met.

- Who should be part of escalation procedures?

See below.

- How should escalation work in practice?

See below.

If answers can be provided to these questions then integration should work.

ESCALATION STRUCTURE

Simple events and incidents can have far-reaching consequences and escalate out of control quickly. There is a common idea that people know what to do when things go wrong (not true) and that they work differently (true). You need the following:

- a team to handle local events;
- a team to handle regional events;
- a team to handle worldwide events;
- training in advance;
- information in advance including pre-planned communications.

Without these an incident, one day, will cause a lot of damage to your revenue, reputation or market share. Don't make this too complicated – it isn't. All that is needed is that there is one person who makes the decision, and that the person has a team to support the process. The exact structure to use varies per company but the objective is the same – consider, decide and act. Each team should have a leader who is responsible for its decision.

A team to handle local events
This team contains representatives of all local functions. This implies business functions as well as support functions such as Legal, Facilities, Human Resources and Communications. The exact representation will vary but this is the minimum.

The business functions will be those responsible for the customer offer (be it product or service) and the functions which should support and resolve incidents.

This team should be led by a senior manager from local management who is available and has the ability and authority to make decisions.

A team to handle regional events
If the company has regional presence then don't assume that one part of the region cares about another – a team is needed to guarantee that things are done as decided. By definition the first priority of a regional sub-team will be its local issues. A regional team should be of the same format as a local one.

A team to handle worldwide events
If ever an event has a worldwide impact then it is pretty serious, so this team will often consist of the senior management board of the company. Its role is simply to orchestrate events on a worldwide level.

Training in advance
What do these teams actually do? It might be obvious to a continuity specialist but it is not necessarily obvious to a functional manager.

These teams need to be trained on how to resolve incidents and events. This does not mean technically resolving them but being capable of driving support teams to a resolution which is in the best interests of the company and its customers. This applies whether the incident is a network outage or a factory fire. They need to understand the scope of an event's impact since this can cover customer satisfaction issues, revenue and profit, reputation, legal liability and other effects. The teams need to know what information sources are available, where these are and how to use them. Their members also need to know when they are part of the team and be locatable, so some kind of notification system needs to be in place:

Prepare a training module that covers:

- team members, their roles and responsibilities;
- how the team will be engaged and when (triggers);
- how the members are contacted and the rota (if applicable);
- how decisions are made and by whom;
- the scope of the team's authority;
- the sources of information available;
- the potential impact of events;
- how to resolve events to customers' satisfaction;
- internal and external communication – when, how and who;
- return to normal action;
- post-mortem and reporting.

Information in advance, including pre-planned communications
Do not expect the managers on these teams to have any information ready – they have a day job as well! BCM Management should prepare the following minimum information to handle events:

- contact lists for all local and official authorities such as fire services, doctors, governments etc.;
- contact lists of all critical staff and management at all levels in the company;
- contact lists for customers;
- recovery and continuity information;
- critical staff rota;
- messages and targeted audience.

These sources of information need to be kept up-to-date and be available on the company network and also offline on DVD. When preparing the information sources (since the above list is not necessarily exhaustive) put yourself in the position of an uninformed manager who has to take over an event and resolve it. What information would **you** need?

The last item (communications) is worth planning in advance in spite of the fact that all events tend to be different. Knowing what sorts of messages would be needed and by whom – particularly the press for major events – can save time. Prepare a matrix showing this messaging as well as showing what types of communication as in this example:

Table 11.3 Communications matrix for major incidents

Contact	Type of message	Message	When
Press	Phone, briefing and press pack	Situation update	As needed or daily
Customers	Phone, email, ticket response	Status	Hourly
Internal staff	Email	Situation update	Daily

Obviously the content of the messages is determined by the situation but this basic planning will help. For example we now know that a press pack is needed and we know that someone will be calling a customer hourly. Therefore someone with the skill and background needs to be available to do this, and this in itself may require coordination between the Communications department and skilled staff. As in most parts of continuity planning this is about planning as much as possible rather than trying to plan and prepare everything in advance.

12 COMMUNICATIONS

Use common sense. Do not drown people with details they do not need and be sure each communication has a target and a desired behavioural change. This is well-known and little practiced. For example why would you give details of issues to people if they cannot help to resolve them or would never be involved? All this will do is waste time. Once you decide on the plan for communications, publish it and tell people in advance what they will get. This also creates authority by formality so it tends to stop people asking for more. If you don't think this works ask yourself why shops have price tickets on items – it creates a formality and stops people haggling. Exactly the same goes for communications plans. Take heed.

The secret to communications is a little and often. There are books on this. However resist the temptation to try to move people from one (usually low) level of competence to another too quickly. Usually speed is more important than quality. Focus communications on what you want people to know to change their behaviour. As an example, does a receptionist need to know how a BIA is run or whether one is done at all? No. However the receptionist does need to know who to call when there is some kind of outage and what procedures are put in place. The inverse is also true. Senior managers need to know that their jobs require them to run BIAs and decide on priorities, but not the details of continuity procedure implementations.

This means that the communications section of the project plan is critical. Table 14.4 is an example of such a plan showing who, when and what.

This is an example only but it must be done and agreed with the sponsor in advance as well, since this will take people's time. Remember that if nothing else you are likely to lose the support of every one of the stakeholders over time, so Communications has a key role in ensuring that the stakeholders can see something for themselves in this. The 'purpose' column can be used for this though in practice it would be more detailed. This communications plan is not to be confused with an external communications plan, which requires the involvement of the formal Communications department. This is for the project, run by the project team and designed to help the project succeed internally. Another big advantage of such a plan is that it makes the team think this through in advance and stops *ad-hoc* communications, which can often be ill-conceived.

Table 12.1 Internal communications matrix

Stakeholder	What communication	When	Comments	Purpose
BCM project sponsor	• Non-detailed project plan	Quarterly	High level detail only	To raise issues and internal selling of the project
	• Status report	Monthly	Including finance status	
	• Milestone presentation	Quarterly	Delivered as a presentation	
Project team	• Status report	Weekly	All issues with and actions/ owners	To keep the project on track
Functional managers	• Status report	Monthly	Delivered 1:1 by BCM manager	To show their responsibilities and actions and help internal selling of the project
	• Issues report	Monthly		
	• Project presentation	Quarterly		
All other staff	• Status presentation	Quarterly	Internal posters, screen savers etc.	Internal communication and selling of the project
	• Training requirements and CBTs	Quarterly		
	• Email and poster reminders	Every six months		

13 TRAINING

A BCM programme has a great impact on every area of an organisation. If it is actually going to work in practice then, for every area of change, there needs to be training. The secrets to training are to tailor the training to the audience, keep it short, repeat it, tailor the message medium to the circumstances and start early. Most of these are self-evident with the possible exception of the last one. Here is an example of a training plan:

Table 13.1 Training plan

Target audience	Training needed	Content	Medium	Duration/ frequency
Senior management	Awareness	What is BCM and why is the company doing it?	• Presentation • Reference card	1 hour/yearly
Functional managers	Awareness	Scenario and procedure design Plan update	• Classpresentation • Overview manual	2 hours/yearly
All staff	Awareness	What is BCM and why is the company doing it?	• Computer-based training – multi-level	4 hours/pass once
Incident management staff	BCM procedures for outages	How BCM integrates into incident management	• Class training • Process map on the web	2 hours/as required (All staff must pass this)

Some key points to note:

- **Keep it short**: You can assume the attention span to be one hour maximum.

- **Repeat it**: Do not try to move people from a low level of skill to a high level in one shot. It will take three at least so have plans to repeat or tailor the levels.

- **Tailor the medium**: Senior managers won't read manuals and functional staff won't follow instructions given in a presentation.

- **Start early**: Don't wait until things are finished to train people. Training should start in phase zero of a project. At the beginning of a project it is clear why it is being done and what people are going to have to do as part of the governance and updating of future plans. Therefore training on these can start even though the project is in its early stages. Training at this stage is part of the selling of a project internally as well.

14 ORGANISATIONAL ISSUES

The management of a BCM project is probably more critical than that of other projects. This is only because the end result is seen as intangible by a lot of people whilst the rest think it is a waste of money. Therefore the communication and milestone side of the project plan take on greater importance. The length of a BCM project is also likely to be well beyond the mean time between reorganisations, so there is a risk that the sponsors will change or disappear.

Here are some simple guidelines which help to manage this situation:

- Never wait more than three months between measurable milestones and results.

- Never present the project plan in detail – it will be far too complicated and no-one will care.

- Work back from the result, not forwards to it (see project management section).

- For every milestone make sure it is the subject of some formal internal communication.

- Communicate with all current and future stakeholders, not just project sponsors (who usually have other things on their minds).

- For all behavioral changes use the sales rule: tell them what you are going to tell them, tell them and then tell them what you told them.

- Never plan tasks more than six months in advance – less if possible.

- Plan the budget over a longer period than this.

- Never give more information than is required for the person receiving it to be influenced. For example never give the project plan detail to Accounting or Operations.

WHERE DOES BCM FIT IN AN ORGANISATION?

The concept of 'availability' is entrenched in the CIA triad of security (confidentiality, integrity and availability). Hence in some circles this is where BCM fits, since it addresses the availability side. This is a mistake. The security role in most companies is fairly passive and usually technical in nature, and treating BCM in this way could mean that continuity does not take its full role in an organisation.

Continuity is a key differentiator as far as the market and customers are concerned and needs to be an inherent characteristic of the products sold. Continuity is also a key market and customer differentiator so where you place BCM in the organisation must be close to these two areas. This means that, at some point in the process of designing a plan, you need to get input from these sources and be sure that the continuity arrangements are reflected in both the company marketing and the customer contracts. Ideally the business continuity management and governance function should report to the board of management directly.

KEEPING THE PLAN UP-TO-DATE

A BCM plan will die over time. People assume that, having developed the plan, that's the end of it – the plan exists. This is true for a very short period – about six months. Not only will the plan die but it won't work perfectly anyway – not first time at least. Therefore it might even provoke stakeholders to wonder why they did the work in the first place.

How do you resolve this? It comes down to a single problem with multiple resolutions. The problem is that the stakeholders think BCM is not their problem. As stated earlier a lot of effort needs to be put into this, especially during the test phase.

There is no single resolution but here are some **dos** and **don'ts**:

Don't:

- Do it by audit alone and impose some audit deadline. This will only ensure last-minute panic or window dressing.

- Do it for them because they won't do it on time or will assume it is not their responsibility.

- Threaten or escalate. All the threats will do is provoke resistance and escalation will bounce back (on you).Impose too many measures. If you do you will get what you measure and history is full of failures in this regard. If you want a measure go for something simple and keep it binary – 'percentage complete' measures are useless. This is a bit like saying your car journey was a success because 99% of the journey was successful, even though you crashed just before getting home. Certain things, such as completion of a BIA, should be mandatory.

- Measure the wrong things. For example measuring the number of procedures tested is less relevant than measuring if they exist, since the simple exercise of developing procedures is already proof of the goodwill you are looking for.

91

- Think it will happen because you said it should or they agreed at some point in the past.

- Keep BCM somehow separate from everyday business. It is not a programme at this stage but has just become part of normal business.

Do:

- Make sure, multiple times, that the stakeholders know it is their problem because it is their business.

- Offer to assist in any phase.

- Make sure job descriptions include BCM actions of some description.

- Make sure senior management share these actions.

- Make sure senior management send supporting/directive messages as needed.

- Audit with a light hand – check that steps are done (that BIAs, threat and risk analyses, scenarios and procedures are developed) and gently chide if not.

- Stress that pre-planning improves overall business efficiency.

- Embed BCM as quickly as possible in normal processes – especially crisis management and incident handling.

- Make sure BCM is embedded in the customer and market offer. This is probably the single most important action. Make sure it is a deliverable in a customer offer or in a product description or service level agreement.

15 BUSINESS CONTINUITY AND THE CLOUD

I have included this very brief section because there is an increasing trend to think that the cloud concept does away with the need for business continuity planning. Nothing could be further from the truth. I will define the cloud by its broad characteristics as imagined by the current state of the art.

A cloud provides on-demand services with no limit on performance or capacity and does this 'somewhere' (users don't need to know where). They ask for something and get it. It never breaks down either. (By 'users' I mean either end-users or the IT department or functional departments that rely on IT.)

This concept actually makes business continuity worse or more difficult to achieve in practice for a number of reasons:

- Business continuity requires people and processes, which are out of the realm of IT, to be defined.

- Business continuity requires a broad consciousness in the organisation to ensure that personnel at every level do their bit.

- Business continuity requires that all threats are looked at and retained risks addressed. The threats and risks are much wider than those seen by IT.

The danger in the cloud is that all the above points are overlooked and the consciousness in an organisation is lost in favour of, 'Don't worry, the cloud does everything and it never breaks down'.

Even assuming that this does not happen, the cloud merely provides the reliability of a single step in a continuity procedure – the ability of IT to do its part of the job.

If we look at the 'disaster recovery' idea in IT, which provides for IT to give continuous service and swap over to another site without losing time or data (I use the common idea of DR here), we could suppose that DR is handled automatically now. Once more nothing is further from the truth.

In this imaginary world we have an IT department which is nothing but a plug in the wall which is infinitely reliable and never breaks down. What happens when the people using the plug can't get into their building? This is one of many severely disruptive scenarios that the cloud cannot solve.

To deal with the cloud concept in a company the lifecycle described in this book should be used and reinforced. This ensures that the idea of the cloud does not overshadow common sense.

16 LESSONS TO LEARN

This chapter is a distillation of some of the key issues in BCM – read it if nothing else. The following list is not exhaustive and apparent contradictions should provoke thought:

- Get a senior level sponsor.
- Make contact with your sponsor twice a month (no more, no less).
- Assume your sponsor will lose interest over time unless you work at it.
- Don't plan the project until full approval is given.
- Note that sending a document is not approval; making a presentation might be.
- Keep the Business Impact Analysis at a business level.
- Remember that IT is rarely a business and usually a resource.
- Use the BIA to prioritise – do not over-analyse.
- Bear in mind that qualitative data is OK for a BIA.
- Get threat and risk information from functional departments too.
- Don't analyse threats if their business impact is low.
- Don't expect any quantitative data when doing the risk analysis.
- Don't have a plan for every risk – ignore some and reduce some.
- Get the people responsible for business to design scenarios for every risk.
- Remember that stakeholders are more important than management.
- Document a step-by-step procedure for every scenario.
- Analyse and desk test every procedure.
- Live test some procedures.
- If a test gives bad performance data, improve the procedure.
- If overall continuity capability is below plan, update customer contracts.
- Make sure BCM procedures are integrated into incident handling.
- Assign an escalation manager to be the single point of contact.
- Develop a communications plan for internal and external use.

- Note that, if you don't have a governance framework, continuity will die fairly soon.
- Start training early in the programme – it is part of communications.
- Remember that the typical attention span is one hour.
- Don't expect the continuity procedures to work flawlessly first time.
- Make sure someone keeps the procedures up-to-date.
- Make sure someone keeps the BIA up-to-date.
- Bear in mind that problem fixing is **not** business continuity planning.
- Remember that high availability is **not** business continuity planning.
- Remember that computers are no substitute for intelligence and planning.

17 CONCLUSION

I have tried to make this subject easy to digest and handle. Business continuity is a subject where the devil is not in the details. No business continuity plan is ever complete or ever works properly first time. It is more important in a company to develop the right attitude towards continuity at all levels than to chase the idea that you can get it right first time. Any plan needs to be exercised and updated regularly so there will be ample opportunity to review things that didn't work first time round.

The 'methodology' presented here looks simple because it is, not because a conscious effort was made to make it simpler than the reality. Everything presented and every point made has worked and does work in practice in every type of business. This does not mean that it will work, unmodified, in every company but the modifications should be cosmetic and will most likely arise due to organisational complexity. The fundamentals, looking at threats and their impact on lines of business and building testable procedures for risk scenarios, are the same for every company.

APPENDIX 1
REFERENCE DATA

There is remarkably little data available showing what are industry accepted ranges for RTO and RPO. The following is a consolidation of data available and it gives a rough idea of what can be expected and what is reasonable. The conclusions that can be drawn are fairly broad only. In any event, whatever business you are in, the RTO and RPO figures are specific to your business and you will soon find out if they are in line with neither the market nor your customer's expectations. However the following table will perhaps serve to give some upper bounds.

The 'percentage of companies' is the key figure. It says that 40 per cent of all companies have RTO figures of less than eight hours, and that typically these would be companies in the supply chain industries where service is usually considered critical.

Table A1.1 Overview of typical RTOs and RPOs for different sectors

What others do – General industry overview

Service class	RTO range	RPO range	Typical application type	Percentage of companies
Real time enterprise	2 hours	zero	Clearing, shipping, core banking	30%
Critical	<8 hours	<4 hours	Invoicing, supply chain	40%
Important	24 hours	12 hours	Office applications	20%
Non-critical	3 days	3 days	Development	10%

Source: Extracted from Gartner, Metagroup and HP
RTO – Recovery Time Objective (revenue loss), RPO – Recovery Point Objective (data loss)

Table A1.2 Typical timescales for continuity strategies

Strategy	Recovery time objective	Advantages	Disadvantages
Repair or rebuild at time of disaster	2–5 months	Lowest cost Fewest resources	Time to recover, reliability, and ability to rehearse
Cold site	1–6 weeks	Cost-effective Time to recover	Testability Detailed plans are difficult to maintain Long-term maintenance costs
Service bureau	1–3 days	Backup for processing critical application, such as payroll	Limited availability for multiple CPU environment
Shippable or transportable equipment	1–3 days	Useful for client/ server computing	Logistical difficulties in regional disaster recovery
Commercial hot site	Less than 1 day	Testability Availability of skilled personnel	Regional disaster risk
Redundant facility	Less than 1 day	Greatest reliability Most control Time to recover	Most expensive Long-term commitment and integrity

Table A1.3 Typical RTOs and RPOs for IT by levels of importance

Classification	Description
IT Service Continuity Level 1 Vital	RTO = 24 hours, RPO = 2 hours Needed for company survival Long-term financial impact Loss of this application would have major impact on ability to continue business Affects entire organisation Severe constraints and legal liabilities
IT Service Continuity Level 2 Critical	RTO = 3 days, RPO = 1 day Essential for company operation and should be run after Priority 1 applications Significant and necessary to maintain control of business operations Affects other departments Moderate to severe financial impact
IT Service Continuity Level 3 Dependent	RTO = 8 days, RPO = 2 days Moderate business impact but Priorities 1 and 2 services will rely on them for data accuracy and support for ongoing production service, or they are more critical than Priority 4 services and should be run after Priorities 1 and 2 Moderate financial impact
IT Service Continuity Level 4 Important	RTO = 15 days, RPO = 2 days Moderate business impact, as with Priority 3, if outage is over a week, and should be run after Priorities 1, 2 and 3 Moderate financial impact

Table A1.3 *(Continued)*

Classification	Description
IT Service Continuity Level 5 Deferrable or do not care	Recovery target (not committed) = about 6 weeks Not needed for immediate company survival and will not be run until the datacentre is fully restored Hardware has to be purchased and necessary space has to be cleared; infrastructure as SAN and LAN has to be set up These applications are for supporting departments and can be suspended for a specified time period without significant impact because of manual backup in place Minimal to no financial impact

APPENDIX 2
TEMPLATES

BIA QUESTIONNAIRE TEMPLATE

This should be completed as follows:

- The current and projected revenue for this business unit. If the actual revenue is not known then agree an estimate. For some business functions providing internal services the revenue may be hidden or expressed as a cost recovery.

- The assets or resources needed to run this business function. This covers all resources – people, hardware, software, services, buildings, infrastructure etc. Anything whose loss affects this business is considered to be a resource for this business function.

- The level of resource needed both short- and long-term. The reason for asking two questions is that losses of resources don't always lead to instant short-term losses of business since there are workarounds which may be possible. So these questions will allow management to express these ideas and provide valuable information for the final report.

- Maximum tolerable unavailability of the resource expressed in hours, days or weeks. This provides an idea of the criticality and the cut-off point.

- The impact in the case of outage. This is the business manager's expression of the revenue loss over time as well as other losses such as customer retention, legal costs etc. This is combined with an expression of when losses start. The values should be quantitative in monetary terms but if not a qualitative value can be substituted (High, Low etc.).

- The threats to the business as perceived by the business manager together with an expression of the state of readiness. There are a number of self-explanatory questions here, including information on historical events and measures in place to avoid the threats and mitigate the risks perceived.

- Weaknesses. Business managers will always have a view on current weaknesses and this should be captured.

Table A2.1 Typical BIA questionnaire template

Line of business	Manager	Email	Date

Revenue per year

Resource required	Short-term	Long-term	Maximum non-availability

Losses (revenue, reputation etc.)	Per hour	Per day	Per week	Per month

Time before loss occurs   Time after which recovery is not possible

Is recovery documented and known?

List major threats to the business

List outages in the last three years

Countermeasures in place to avoid outage

Weaknesses seen

Other comments?

THREAT/RISK QUESTIONNAIRE TEMPLATE

Table A2.2 BCM threat /risk exposure questionnaire

Name of respondent

Position/area of responsibility

E-mail address

Provide a brief description on the assets (infrastructure) you protect

Which business services do the assets support?

Specify annual budget assigned to your department for threat/risk mitigation (GBP, USD)

Threats perceived
Specify major threats that affect the assets you protect. Focus on threats representing major residual risk to the assets (i.e. consider also the strength of countermeasures in place when selecting the threats). List top-priority threats and validate the completeness using the threat catalogue.

Table A2.3 Table for summarising threats and countermeasures

Threat title	Description	Countermeasures in place	Estimated periodicity of occurrence

---

Outage/incident history for the last three years

Specify major outages/incidents affecting the respective assets you protect in the period of the last three years.

Table A2.4 Table for summarising outages over last three years

Outage/incident description (Describe nature and extent of the outage/incident.)	Degraded service provided during the outage? (Add brief description of the degraded service.)	Financial impact	Recovery scenario description (Specify how the assets were recovered, in what time and at what the cost.)
	☐ Yes ☐ No Description:		
	☐ Yes ☐ No Description:		

Outage Preparedness
The purpose of this section is to determine the level of preparedness to mitigate outages and identify major weaknesses in this area.

Table A2.5 Summary sheet for contingency plans

Are there contingency/recovery plans and procedures documented for these assets?

☐ Yes

☐ No

Specify:

Are those plans and procedures currently up-to-date?

☐ Yes

☐ No

Specify:

How are those plans and procedures communicated and tested?

Specify major dependencies you have on other departments/services which could affect your capabilities. Are these dependencies documented?

Are there other areas of weakness (not specified yet in this questionnaire) which you would like to improve (if you would have the budget)?

INDEX